JEWISH THOUGHT IN CONTEXT

Studies in the relationship of Jewish and general thought

Rabbi Dr. Shimon Dovid Cowen

Published by
the Institute for Judaism and Civilization, Melbourne
& Australian Centre for Jewish Civilization, Monash University
with the assistance of the
Monash University Publications Grants Committee

For Miriam

Jewish Thought in Context,
Second, revised edition
© 1998 by Rabbi Dr. S.D. Cowen

Monographs in Judaism and Civilization
ISSN 1441-1784
No. 1. *Jewish Thought in Context*
ISBN 0 9585933 0 2

Cover graphic: Simcha Fetter

For information and further copies please contact:
Institute for Judaism and Civilization,
88 Hotham Street
East S. Kilda, Victoria 3183
Australia
Telephone 61-3-9522 8222
Facsimile 61-3-9522 8266

CONTENTS

INTRODUCTION

Providence has furnished one with certain teachers - if not personal teachers, then those who became one's teachers through the study of their oeuvres and, in some cases, through extensive contact with *their* students. In my case, these teachers were, in the realm of secular thought, the modern German philosopher Theodor Wiesengrund Adorno, and in Jewish thought, the Chassidic master, the Lubavitcher Rebbe, Rabbi Menachem Mendel Schneerson. Whilst the positions of Jewish philosophy came to be my conviction, I did not want - by an insight of Chassidic thought itself - wholly to jettison that which I had learnt from Adorno. This insight is that, also from a Torah point of view, elements of truth are to be found in the arts and sciences "external" to Torah. The task is, through the light of Torah, critically to extract these elements, which in turn will serve to illuminate Torah further.

It is a common hermeneutic insight that one reads the past through the present, in this case through one's teachers of the present. That need not relativize the writing of history or the history of ideas. From a Jewish point of view, the chain of Torah tradition, whilst being made up of a great number of individual links, forms a single alignment and a single focus all the way back to the one revelatory experience of Sinai. So too, if Torah can verify certain elements in secular philosophies of the present, then these will also add an authoritative framework.

When, therefore, we set out constructions of the history of Jewish and non-Jewish thought, it is clearly through the lenses of those teachers of the present, Adorno and Rabbi Menachem Mendel Schneerson. The historical figures which fill those constructions, who are selected for comparison - Maimonides with the Christian thinkers, Augustine and Aquinas, the Maharal of Prague with the Renaissance figures, Bacon, Machiavelli, Shakespeare, Rabbi Schneur Zalman of Liadi with Hegel, and the Lubavitcher Rebbe with Adorno - are significant *for* the philosophies of Rabbi Schneerson and Adorno. Thus, this comparative history of ideas "begins" and "ends" with them. The figure of Rabbi J.B. Soloveitchik has been added in the last chapter, even though his thought is not in the *specific* tradition within Judaism from which Rabbi Schneerson's thought receives, in order to explain to a Jewish audience the convergence of his and Rabbi Schneerson's positions.

Questions "beg" themselves. We have in this monograph sought to show certain parallels and differences between Jewish and non-Jewish thought of the same epochs. But how do Jewish and non-Jewish thought *interact*? From a Jewish point of view, what uses does Jewish thought make of non-Jewish thought? Pursuit of this question would have led us to relate Maimonides to the Arabic neo-Aristotelian Averroes, rather than to Augustine and Aquinas, who respectively preceded him by many hundreds of years and lived after him. Or alternatively this question might have been approached in connection with analyses of the notion of *Zeitgeist*: if philosophies are symptomatic of the issues of their time, then conceivably we could speak of relationships amongst thinkers, who did not even know each other. In fact, Jewish mystical thought itself has much to say on this topic through the concepts of *shviras hakeilim* (the "breaking of the vessels") and *avodas habirurim* ("the service of extraction and refinement"). All these issues, important as they are, are, however, not treated here.

What this monograph does seek to do is to relate the secular philosophical concepts of subject and object to their counterparts in Jewish thought; and to do this historically through Adorno's view of the changing philosophical relationship of subject and object, for which strong parallels exist in the history of Jewish thought. The translation of subject and object into Jewish terms thus allows the construction of parallel histories of Jewish and general thought. Within these we have made a series of comparative studies, which should bring out fundamental differences between Jewish and general thought.

The possibility of a translation of subject and object into Jewish terms follows from the fact that both Jewish and non-Jewish thought have philosophical concerns. Both address a *subject*, man or the human mind, which relates to an *object*, reality. The difference between them, however, lies in the question: what is relating to what? What is man or mind and what is reality?

For Adorno, as indeed for history of general thought, the meaning of the subject- object relationship is that of one piece of creation, *mind*, dealing with another part of creation, (non-mental) reality or nature. For Jewish philosophy, as expressed in the work of the Lubavitcher Rebbe, the subject is also man, who thinks, speaks and most significantly (as in Adorno) *acts*. But *that which* is thinking through the apparatus of the mind is the *soul*, the essential man. The soul of man and woman, at one level, is called the *tzelem Elokim*, the likeness of G-d. In the Jewish people, specifically it is termed the G-dly soul. The soul is G-dly; it is a "piece" of G-dliness. That which it thinks about, or relates to - external reality or nature - is also G-dliness. For the true reality of nature is the G-dliness which constantly animates it from nothingness.

In short, the subject-object relationship in general thought is that of creation - created intellect - thinking about creation, nature, reality. In Jewish thought, it is G-dliness - the soul which enclothes itself in the mind - thinking about G-dliness, the animating principle of Creation. The subject of general philosophy, "created intellect", possesses those operations, delineated by philosophy and psychology alike, of which the brain is finitely capable, with which it was *created*. The logical, operational structure of the mind does enable it to construct an infinite progression; it does not enable it to comprehend something which is at once blue and not blue. The natural or created character of mind also relates to the mind's assimilation of the phenomena of creation to form analogies, constructs, metaphors. If the style of a person is described as "wooden", it is because it is analogous to the rigidity found in wood; if some poetry is found to be "crystalline", it is because it possesses the elaborate symmetries of a crystal. Wood and crystals are found in creation. But intellect cannot it construct, even by mutation, the likeness of something for which no materials or concepts exist in the creation.

In the soul, on the other hand, and specifically in the spiritual apparatus of the Jewish people, there are a number of "levels". Chassidic and Kabalistic thought discern five levels in the soul. In general, these divide into three general levels, which in turn are able to relate to different levels or dimensions of G-dliness in the "macrocosm": immanent, transcendent and quintessential or absolute G-dliness - to be elaborated in the coming chapters. Whilst the mind is naturally equipped *by itself* to comprehend the manifestation of immanent G-dliness, it does not by itself comprehend those manifestations of G-dliness which transcend the creation. Nevertheless, the mind's "spiritual" eye, the soul, can employ thought or speech to address these manifestations, even if it does so negatively or paradoxically.

Adorno, whose father was Jewish and who worked in a secularly Jewish intellectual milieu in Frankfurt before, and in New York during, the war, is a secular thinker, the heir to a great tradition beginning with Hegel. And yet it seems in his work that he too was, by some sort of reference to Jewish themes of transcendence, of the prohibition on (graven) images and so forth, seeking to leave the orbit *(Bahn)* of general thought. In fact, he remained fully within it; but his thought offers us the means to explain Jewish thought to the secular mind.

This monograph was developed under the generous and tolerant auspices of two institutions. The Kollel Menachem Lubavitch of Melbourne, under the direction of Rabbis Y.D. and C.T. Groner, afforded me the time to write it. The occasion to conceive and present its thoughts was given by the Australian Centre for Jewish Civilisation, Monash University, under the direction of Professor Bernard Rechter, first in a special series of public lectures and then as a course. I thank my students in this course for assisting me through clarification of its ideas.

CHAPTER 1

THE TRANSLATION OF TERMS

In order to relate Jewish thought to the history of general thought, its "context", useful secular terms can be found in the work of the modern German philosopher, T. W. Adorno, who is situated in a tradition deriving from Hegel. These are "subject", "object" *and* "praxis" *(the interaction of subject and object). The terms in* Jewish *thought which correspond to these are* the spiritual entity of the Jewish people, "transcendent" G-dliness and the service ("avoda") of the Jewish people. *Within this translation of terms - and based on a schema, in Adorno's thought, of the history of ideas as the changing relationship of subject and object - it is possible to discern parallel histories of Jewish and general thought.*

We shall be concerned with four common periods of Jewish and general thought: (i) the medieval epoch in which Maimonides' focus on the transcendent aspect of G-dliness parallels the metaphysical, object-centred doctrines of Augustine and Aquinas; (ii) the Renaissance, in which the Maharal of Prague, with his emphasis upon the spiritual entity of the Jewish people, parallels the Renaissance preoccupation with the subject, man; (iii) the late Enlightenment philosophy, in which Rabbi Schneur Zalman of Liadi portrayed absolute or quintessential G-dliness as uniting immanent and transcendent dimensions of G-dliness "analogously" to the Hegelian concept of the Absolute as the identical subject-object; and (iv) the interest of the contemporary Jewish philosophies of Rabbi Menachem Mendel Schneerson and Rabbi J.B. Soloveitchik in the individual as an agent or partner of absolute G-dliness, to which corresponds Adorno's own notion of the individual as the author of the social Whole or "Praxis".

1. "Subject", "object" and the philosophical epochs of general thought

Subject, object, praxis

In the European, or more specifically German, tradition of philosophy going back to Hegel, we find that the most basic terms of philosophy are "subject" and "object". "Subject", in the work of these thinkers, refers to the knowing, interpreting mind, the human mind. "Object" refers to the reality, which the subject, the mind, contemplates. It is "reality", construed variously as substance by Hegel, or by Kant as the "thing in itself", that which is "before" the cognitive activity of the subject comes to it.

The "idealist" philosophies of Kant and Hegel present quite different views of the way in which the subject comes to its understanding of reality, of the object. What they have in common is that they see the relationship of subject and object as one of *thought* and reality. They are interested in the phenomena of mental activity. Whilst it is true that Hegel saw the development of mind as having concrete expression in history, his thought is yet idealist rather than materialist inasmuch as all concrete phenomena are simply the external expression of the development of mind.

It was Karl Marx, who following in many ways in the direction of Hegelian thought, transposed the relationship of subject and object into the realm of concrete activity: *praxis*. Praxis quite simply means action. It is comprehended as taking place on the plane of the real, the objective. However different mind and body, thought and being, might be, they still occupy, and function on, the one material plane. Thought - subject - itself has a material interest.

Thus, for Marx, even in his early works, subject is not the abstract entity "mind". It is man as a social and economic being. Where for idealist thought, the object was still a metaphysical concept, being or substance, the "thing in itself", for Marx it is absolutely concretely: nature - the stuff of economic, productive activity. It is true, as we shall see, that already the Renaissance had "secularized" metaphysical reality. What for the religious middle ages, was the Divine order of being, became in the Renaissance "nature". But this was a nature, which the early modern subject was interested to *know*, not with which it saw itself as concretely *interacting*.

Adorno, whilst working some hundred years after Marx began to formulate his philosophy, is yet strongly in the tradition of Marx and the Marxian transposition of Hegelian terms. His work incorporates both the existential individualism and humanism of Marx's early work and the macro-social and economic perspectives of the Mature Marx. What interests us most here is Adorno's understanding of the relationship of subject and object as one of *praxis*.

According to Adorno, not only is the human being's productive economic work, as signaled by Marx, a praxis, a concrete interaction with nature, driven by material interests, meeting nature on its own terms. The same can be said about human *thought*. In Adorno's words, "thought is a doing". In this he goes beyond Marx. For Marx thought - the realms of conscious production such as art, literature and philosophy were simply an ideological *reflex* of real social and economic work relationships: culture is that which reflects and reinforces the supremacy of a particular class in the relations of *production*. For Adorno on the other hand, thought is not simply a reflex of economic activity; it is itself a more primary and seminal form of activity. Economic forms grow out of - reflect - it more than vice-versa: philosophy, one could say, is the fount of economics.

Going back to the earliest times, the stance of the subject, man or mind, vis-à-vis the object, nature, is formed by a drive for mastery prompted by insecurity. Man, placed in the midst of nature, is afraid, feels his own existence jeopardized, and responds by wanting to control nature. There is, therefore, primarily a *practical* relationship between man and nature. *Thought*, the decisive hallmark man, becomes a mode, and the primary mode, of the subject's approach to the control of the object. This instrumental motive in, and characteristic quality of, thought finds its apotheosis in the Enlightenment; and human intellectual history is the prehistory of the Enlightenment. Hence the title of Adorno and Max Horkheimer's seminal work, *The Dialectic of the Enlightenment*[1]. It is a story of the coming to self-consciousness of thought in the Enlightenment as the intellectual praxis of the domination of nature. It does this inasmuch as it systematically describes and analyses the phenomena of nature, rendering them into categories and relationships which serve their scientific and technological mastery. This is what Adorno calls variously "subjective", "identifying" and "instrumental" reason; and in other places, the "subject philosophy".

A phrase of *The Dialectic of the Enlightenment* guides the reconstruction of its argument for a schema of four phases of human intellectual history in terms of the changing relationship of the subject to the object:

Pure, natural existence, animal and vegetative, formed for civilization the greatest danger. Mimetic, mythical, metaphysical [elsewhere described as "scholastic"] modes of dealing [Verhaltensweisen] appear one after the other, as superseded ages of the world[2].

---

[1] References here are to the German edition, *Dialektik der Aufklärung; philosophische Fragmente*, Frankfurt am Main: Fischer, 1973 (original edition 1947). All quotations are translations of the present author from the German.

[2] *Op. cit.*, p. 31.

That which supersedes the last of these is a fourth epoch, the Enlightenment, with its inception in the Renaissance, in which the subject becomes aware of itself as the arbiter and patterner of meaning. It is qualitatively different from the preceding epochs of thought, here described as mimetic (pertaining to the cultural epoch of *animism*), mythical (relating to classical Greek and Roman thought) and metaphysical-scholastic (relating to the essentially religious outlook of the Middle Ages). The common characteristic of these first three epochs is that the subject experiences itself not as that which *posits*, but rather as the *recipient* of the truth of, the object. These epochs bear out in different ways a sense of the "priority" of the object.

Priority of the object

Mimetic thought is already a mode of the subject's dealing with its object, nature. It is associated variously with "magic" and "sacrifice", where the subject, barely aware of itself as an agent separate from nature, seeks to invoke and entreat nature through *mimesis*, literally "imitation". That is, the subject approaches the object, not by seeking to apprehend it, but rather by seeking to make itself *like*, by seeking an "affinity" with, it - as *it* is.

> Magic, like science, is based on goals, but it pursues them through mimesis, not through progressive distance from the object[3].

The subject's imitation, and through this its evocation of the powers, of nature in animism and, on the other hand, its self-conscious construction and manipulation of nature in the scientific philosophy of the Enlightenment are the two polar extremes of the historical development. In animism there is a

---

[3] *Ibid.*, p.13.

fluid identity of subject and object, form and content: the subject is *given over* to the object.

In the next epoch, that of mythic thought - and since this is how Adorno denotes the *classical* Greek and Roman epoch, he presumably includes with it the philosophical cosmologies of Greek and Roman thought - are to be found the seeds of the Enlightenment. It is the beginning of the subject's active and manipulative stance towards the object. The spontaneity of the animistic conception of nature and the spirit of self-surrender accompanying it, are replaced by the cosmological patterning of nature in myth. Mythological thought delineates the themes of cycle *[Kreislauf]* and destiny *[Schicksal]*, elements of an eternal, ordered reality. Mythical thought is schematic, representing the hidden (as yet unselfconscious) subject's patterning of reality. It is the "transformation of the sacrifice into subjectivity"[4] without, however, the subject's awareness of itself as the agent which brings about this ordering of reality. Mythic thinking renders objective reality into a structured symbolic whole; as such it is the prototype of the scientific thinking of the modern Enlightenment - only without awareness of itself as the subject which *creates* that order.

The *Dialectic of the Enlightenment* speaks little of the following - the medieval, *metaphysical* - epoch *per se*. It is more interested in its aspect of continuity with myth. Like myth, the medieval, theological world view accepted a fundamental *objectivity* in the picture of the order of reality; it has not yet consciously made the subject the controlling ordering principle. Thus, together with cultural vestiges of animism and myth, the doctrines of the "Catholic hierarchy" fall before the consciously subjective, man- and mind-centred reason of the Enlightenment. In all these previous thought forms there vanishes, as mythological, every devotion

---

[4] *Ibid.*, p.52.

[self-orientation], which considered itself objective, as established in the [order of] thing[s][5].

Whilst Adorno here is principally concerned to see the common aspect in mythology and medieval metaphysics from the point of view of the programme of "disenchantment" and "demythologization" undertaken by the Enlightenment, the difference between the two phases can also be discerned in the *Dialectic of the Enlightenment*. This is that, whereas myth represents the subject's ordering of the object, it yet, as noted, involves the concealment of the subject's activity from itself: it is the birth of subjectivity, without any awareness of itself as subjectivity. On the other hand, the medieval metaphysical and theological world view *reflects* upon general categories of objectivity, that is, upon the mind-like character of reality. A table of mental, metaphysical - not interpretative, cosmological or mythological - categories describe the organization of reality: but this is a subjectivity which is yet *attributed* to the object. Adorno writes elsewhere that for Anselm's "ontological proof", the *mental* concept *[Begriff]* is "true"[6], that is, held to be *objectively inherent* in reality. There is, in other words, a notion of the subject - consciousness - as the medium of understanding, but in a way of *reflection* of the intrinsic, organizing principle of the object.

Phases of the subject philosophy

One does not find in the *Dialectic of the Enlightenment* any schematic differentiation of the phases of modern thought, as one does with pre-modern thought. Based on this text, and on Adorno's other writings, however, one can delineate the following stages: Renaissance, Enlightenment and the

---

[5] *Ibid.*, p.84.
[6] Theodor W. Adorno, *Negative Dialektik*, Frankfurt am Main: Suhrkamp, 1966, p. 394.

contemporary philosophy of the individual as expressed in Adorno's own thought.

In the *Dialectic of the Enlightenment*, the Renaissance figure of Francis Bacon stands as the symbol of the birth of the "subject philosophy". His notion, that we must know nature in order to have dominion over it, is its manifesto. True and useful knowledge is that which is gathered and construed by, and which ultimately serves the efficacy of, the subject: Bacon is the herald of the ethos of modern science and technology. At the same time there is a certain "loneliness" in the Baconian subject. It looks out over nature, stands over against it. Perhaps, Cartesian dualism also expresses this solitude and separation of the subject in the Renaissance.

The Enlightenment pursues and develops the subject philosophy of the Renaissance, preeminently in Kant's philosophy, where the subject is seen as manifestly constitutive of knowledge of the object. Yet in Hegel, who may be viewed either as a late Enlightenment thinker, or at least an immediate heir of the Enlightenment, there is a significant turning. Hegel's philosophy takes up the historical contribution of Kant's philosophy, but also, in Adorno's view, rectifies a defect in the Kantian philosophy: the "sundering"[7] of subject and object, which produces a gulf between the "phenomenon" of consciousness and objectivity, the "thing in itself" *(Ding an sich)*. Hegel, in introducing the concept of the unified or identical subject-object, presents the dialectical interaction of subject and object and restores the distinct value of the objective, real moment. This "objective turning in Hegel is the restitution of the speculative metaphysics which was shattered by the criticist [philosophy of Kant]"[8]. Hegel maintains the

---

[7] Theodor W. Adorno, Drei Studien zu Hegel, Gesammelte Schriften, Bd. 5 Frankfurt am Main: Suhrkamp, 1971, p. 255.
[8] Ibid., p. 277-78.

moments of subjectivity and objectivity as they have also been distinguished from one another, and yet grasps them as mediated through one another[9].

The subject does not simply picture the object and understand it in terms of its own categories: it works with and in the object. It participates and engages in the reality of the object. This was brought out fully in Hegel's revolutionary pupil, Karl Marx. For Marx, as noted above, the work of the subject with the object is understood concretely, not simply as cognitive, but as a *praxis*, a doing. The subject, man, is engaged through production in the object, nature. Man and nature are joined by the nexus of historical modes of production. The powers of nature are drawn into, and respond to, the formative activity of man.

Adorno's own thought presents a third phase of the subject philosophy. Adorno takes over the notion of subject-object Praxis from Hegel and Marx, namely that subject and object, man and nature, are "sides" of a composite process. This process, for the Mature Marx, as in its idealist form in Hegel, was, however, a reality which overarched and subsumed the individual. For Adorno, on the other hand, individuals do not simply illustrate historical, social and economic realities. The individual is the *author* of the process, of the total reality described as subject-object. Individuals create a whole which either estranges or emancipates them. Here is the most highly developed sense of the human *agency* of the formation and change of the order of man and nature, Praxis, embracing society, economy and culture. "Praxis" comes less to signify the *order* of the human, social engagement than the transformative, creative activity of individuals, by which such orders are *brought into being*.

---

9 *Ibid.*, p. 256.

In summary, working with the terms subject and object, and their changing philosophical relationship we can draw from Adorno's writing three epochal modes of the relationship of subject and object, bringing forth the priority of the object: (i) the mimetic mode corresponding to the epoch of animism, (ii) the mythic mode corresponding to the classical, Greek and Roman epoch, and (iii) the metaphysical or scholastic mode of the middle ages. Within the fourth epoch, that of the subject philosophy, in which the philosophical praxis of the subject becomes conscious of itself, we can delineate another three periods: (a) the subject philosophy of the Renaissance, (b) the subject-object process in the work of Hegel and Marx and (c) the contemporary philosophy of the individual as author of this process, in Adorno's own work. Let us now proceed to the Jewish translation of the terms, subject, object and praxis, and see how Jewish thought relates to the epochal changes in the relationship of subject and object in general thought.

2. Jewish thought: relationships to the Divine

The Jewish people, G-d and the service of G-d

The modernity of Chassidic thought, as we shall explain at greater length, is found in the fact that it consciously relates to the Divine through man. That "man" is the spiritual faculty in human beings, the complex of the soul. The distinguishing characteristic of all humanity, that to which the biblical expression of the making of man "in the image of G-d" *(tzelem Elokim)* refers, is the intellectual soul[10]. Its *spirituality* consists its being equipped to turn its gaze "upwards", to contemplate G-dliness as the source and significance of all phenomena in creation. Intrinsically this human intellect is independent of material concerns, of the dominion of instinct and emotion.

---

[10] See Rabbi Menachem Mendel Schneerson, *Likkutei Sichos* (Kehos, N.Y.), Vol 15, p.58ff

The ability to disregard the Divine, and to look "downwards" - seeking to understand or become involved in the material creation without any reference to a Divine source - derives from the same G-dly quality or likeness in man. He/she is "like G-d, knowing good and bad"[11]. Frequently, we find that intellect has been influenced to take its premises from sentiment, from a predisposed will. It becomes the rationale of feeling.

The specific significance of the Jewish people, within humanity as a whole, is that Jews have a spiritual property which *fixes* the direction of intellect towards G-dliness. This is related to the concept of the *chosenness* of the Jewish people, a phenomenon which occurred at the exodus from Egypt and the giving of the Torah. It signifies a special bonding between the Jewish people and G-dliness, in that a spiritual nexus to G-dliness was, so to speak, implanted within, and became part of, the Jewish spiritual make-up. The intensity of this bond is expressed through the body of six hundred and thirteen mitzvos - literally commandments, etymologically connoting *connections* - incumbent upon the Jewish people. Even an unobservant Jew latently possesses evoked. General humanity, on the other hand, is bound, biblically, by seven general mitzvos, the Noahide laws. The righteous of the nations have an attachment to the Jewish people and to Torah in that it is Jewish spirituality - the "light to the nations", which is first a light within, and to, the Jewish soul itself - that pilots and helps to actualize the *tzelem Elokim*, the image of G-d, in mankind. The Jewish people represent, in the sense of focussing, the Spiritual subjectivity of mankind. The Jewish people represent, in the sense of focussing, the Spiritual subjectivity of mankind.

The "Object" of this spiritual subject, the Jewish people, is not the physical creation, nature, as such, but that which

---

[11] *Genesis*, 3:5. See also *Likkutei Sichos*, Vol. 19, p. 280-81 fn. 45.

engenders, brings creation *into existence.* This is transcendent G-dliness, the creative foundation of being. As Maimonides states in his thirteen principles of the faith, while all existence depends upon G-d, G-d is in no way to be equated with any level or facet of existence, or bound to existence in any level or facet of existence, or bound to existence in any way, for G-d creates existence. Not even the term "exists", in the way this term applies to the creation, can be applied to G-d as transcendent Creator. Chassidic philosophy speaks of a transcendent G-dliness as the life force of all existence and it describes the notion of creation *ex nihilo* - something from nothing *(yesh mei'ayin)* - as a constant process. Accordingly, were this process to cease, even for a moment, all existence would revert to nothingness. In this sense the true being of all existence is G-dliness, but creation does not participate in, or describe, G-dliness. The G-dly enlivening life-force is neither pantheistic nor panentheistic: it is transcendental world. This could not be so, in view of the purpose of man in creation, elaborated by Chassidic thought: the making of the material world, specifically, into a vessel for transcendent G-dliness.[12] But in this task, the Jewish people addresses primarily not the world, physical creation, but rather the "Principle" of the world, G-d, Who makes and remakes it from second to second. In seeking to make the world into such a vessel, it necessarily invokes, or participates in, the powers of Its Creator to do so.

Notwithstanding the spiritual content of subject and object in Jewish theology, their relationship is thus a worldly and practical one. It is called *avoda*, literally "work", more generally the *service* of G-d. It is analogous to the concept of *praxis* in the secular philosophy, which portrays to the subject's relations to nature as one of formative, productive work,

---

[12] At a deeper level, to be discussed in chapter 4, it is absolute G-dliness *(Atzmus)* which creates.

through which it seeks to elicit the powers of nature. The task of the service of the Jewish people - in conjunction with the civilizing work of mankind through fulfillment of the Noahide laws[13] - is to reveal the powers of the Creator in the creation.

There are several modalities or dimensions in this service. The first of these is the "apprehension" of a *transcendent* level of G-dliness, which is found "beyond" beyond creation and created intellect. This apprehension is achieved through the intellect's "negation" of intellect: in terms of Chassidic thought "*bitul*", or self-nullification. Another modality of this service is the drawing down of this transcendent G-dliness into the realm of *immanence* within the creation: in the life of the Jewish people and thereby into the creation as a whole. There is a further service in the apprehension of the level of G-dliness termed here "absolute" or "quintessential", which embraces and unifies both transcendent and immanent G-dliness. This is "true" G-dliness, Which it is the task of Jewish people to reveal in creation. Finally there is the service of the invocation of this power of G-dliness Itself, so as to reconstitute and renew the creation, in such a way as to allow absolute G-dliness to be revealed in the creation. This is connected in a special way with the individual, and it completes the facets of the *avoda*, the spiritual service of the Jewish people.

The dialectical relationship and sequence of these dimensions of Divine service are to be construed and studied particularly in the work of Rabbi Menachem Mendel Schneerson. Here is not the place for presentation of this dialectic. The delineation of these dimensions, by themselves, of the relationship of the

---

[13] The seven general laws referred to above: the prohibitions of idolatry, blasphemy, murder, theft, sexual immorality, specific forms of cruelty to animals, and failing to establish processes of justice.

spiritual subject to the Divine, however, enables us to portray epochs of Jewish thought paralleling those in Adorno's schema of the history of general thought.

The doctrines of transcendent G-dliness
The first of these epochs - which Adorno termed "mimetic" in the sense in which object overwhelms the subject, which can seek only to make itself "like" the object - finds its counterpart in the Jewish epoch of prophecy. The epoch of prophecy runs from biblical times through to the end of the first Temple and the return from exile to the land of Israel with the building of the second Temple, and the prophets, Ezra and Nechemia. The "Great Assembly" contained a number of prophets and the last of the figures of the Great Assembly was Shimon HaTzaddik, a watershed figure who marks the end of prophecy and the beginning of the Mishnaic and Talmudic era.

The point of analogy between the epoch which Adorno terms "mimetic" and prophecy, is that the cognitive faculty of intellect is in a state of self-nullification to its object. In terms of Adorno's schema, prophecy embodies the notion of the absorption of the subject's faculties in the object: it is a visionary, rather than cognitive, quality which makes the prophet a vehicle for prophecy. Thus, prophecy - which produced the written Torah, the twenty four books of TaNaCH, pre-eminent among which, and the hub of all Torah, the Five Books of Moses, is not *drawn through* the filter of intellect. Prophecy "wears" the faculties of the prophet. It is true that prophecy is achieved through certain kinds of contemplation, but not through the ordinary "rational", cognitive faculties of intellect. As Maimonides writes with regard to the breastplate of the High Priest : " . . . and *ru'ach hakodesh* ["divine inspiration"] enclothes itself in the Kohen and he looks at it in the *vision* of prophecy."[14] Prophecy accesses a realm which is beyond creation: it finds truth in a realm which is that of transcendent G-dliness, just as Torah itself is something "beyond" the world, "G-d's wisdom". It is not something that the cognitive spiritual faculty in man can achieve, but rather a faculty which accesses the transcendent: it is G-d Who speaks, or in the terms of Maimonides' sixth principle, confers prophecy upon man.

Corresponding to mythic thought, or the cosmological character of classical Greek and Roman thought, is the oral Torah. It was given with the written Torah, as its commentary, but is substantially "unfolded" in the Mishnaic and Talmudic epoch, which follows upon prophecy. Its characteristic is its "rationality". The difference between it and the prophetic texts, the written Torah, is expressed in halachah: one has not fulfilled the commandment of learning Torah with the study of the oral law, unless one has understood what one has learnt, whereas with the written law, one has fulfilled the commandment simply by reading it, even without understanding. Nevertheless, the "oral Torah" bases itself upon the Written Torah. That is to say, the function of the oral law is to explicate and elucidate that which is cryptically stated in the Written torah. It is a body of received interpretation of the Written law and the study of the Oral law is a logical and rational inquiry within the premises and dicta transmitted by it.

Because, moreover, the oral Torah receives from, and assumes the foundations of, prophecy, it did not therefore require the cosmological labours of classical thought which made a new start, being indifferent, if not hostile, to the "animistic" past. It was not concerned to delineate a cosmos; its cosmos was the world of prophecy. Its task was

---

[14] *Mishneh Torah, Hilchos K'lei HaMikdosh* 10:11.

intellectually to provide the rational elucidation of that which had been received through prophecy. That is why a statement such as that of Julius Guttmann[15], that Rabbinic Judaism had a poorly developed philosophical sense is fundamentally mistaken. There was no need for the Rabbis philosophically to depict a cosmos. The structures of objective being, which the Greek and Roman mind sought intellectually to establish, was in the Jewish experience the reality of prophecy. There was no need to say anything new or foundational about this but simply to elucidate it, whether in the traditions of law (Halachah) or mysticism (Kabalah). The oral law and its tradition represents the spiritually informed intellect's explication of the objective, transcendent realm of revelation. Revelation is the *expression*, the communication of the transcendent G-d.

It has been noted that the common feature of the three epochs of thought, which Adorno called the "mimetic", "mythical" and medieval "metaphysical" epochs, is that all of them set forth the priority of the object: the subject is not yet aware of itself as constitutive of its world, but experiences itself in various degrees as receptive of the object. Analogous to the priority of object in non-Jewish thought, we find in Jewish thought that G-dliness is conceived principally in its transcendent aspect. The difference with medieval philosophy is that it begins not so much to describe as to *reflect* upon the existence of an objective reality. Analogies to this reflection upon object are to be found in Jewish medieval philosophy in a distinct grouping of Jewish philosophers, which appears as a new genre in Jewish thought. Rabbi Saadia Gaon, Maimonides, Nachmanides, Abarbanel, Rabbi Yosef Albo, and Rabbi Yehudah HaLevi are examples of this new species of

---

[15] *Philosophies of Judaism* (transl. D.W. Silverman) N.Y: Schocken, 1973, p.45.

Jewish thought which is overtly philosophical in style. The philosophical reflection upon transcendent G-dliness is found *par excellence* in the teachings of Maimonides concerning Divine attributes. It is expressed in the notion of *y'dias hashlila*, knowledge that G-dliness negates any apprehension or description whatsoever which the mind can produce. Just as non-Jewish medieval metaphysical and theological thought makes philosophical, renders into mental terms, the sense of absorption of subject into the greater metaphysical reality of the object, so does Maimonides make philosophical the sense of the creaturely intellect's nullification to G-dliness in its transcendent aspect, in terms of a notion of the "negative" knowledge of G-d. Intellect apprehends, but only negatively, by its own self-negation.

Jewish medieval thought contains the *beginnings*[16] of Jewish philosophy, because earlier epochs did not need to reflect upon or to demonstrate the existence G-dliness, since they experienced it directly in prophecy and in the internal elucidation of prophecy in the oral tradition. Only the further descent of generations into relative spiritual darkness would *require* a philosophical *Guide for the Perplexed*.

Immanent and absolute (quintessential) G-dliness

Jewish thought parallels subsequently the beginnings of Enlightenment thought in the *Renaissance*, with its elevation of the subject to self-conscious construction of the object. Jewish thought does this by moving into the sphere in which intellect *can* speak *positively* about G-dliness, but without in any way infringing monotheism. Here it speaks about G-dliness as it functions not transcendently, but *immanently* in creation. In

---

[16] The issue of the relation of Philo to the Rabbinic, Torah tradition is not discussed here.

relation to the concept of immanent G-dliness, the Talmud states, "Just as the soul fills the body, so does the Holy One, blessed be He, fill the world"[17]. In other words, as distinct from the unlimited G-dliness which engenders each and every particular existing thing constantly into being, there is also an indwelling or immanent G-dliness which enlivens and constitutes, so to speak, the "soul" of each particular being. It is the Maharal of Prague, who pioneers this new emphasis on G-dliness in immanence, which Kabalistic and Chassidic thought calls the *Shechina* or the *indwelling* Divine Presence. He points the way to a comparison with the secular Renaissance subject philosophy, in that he focuses upon the *Jewish people* as bearers of the "spiritual form" *within* creation[18].

The further development of modern philosophy is seen by Adorno in the philosophy of Hegel, the essential culmination of Enlightenment thought. In his work there is posited the ideal of the unity of "subject" and "object", "thought" and "nature", in the appropriation of nature essential to the fulfillment of man, as this is set out in the *Philosophy of Right*. The *Jewish* notion of the accomplished "identity" or "unity" of subject and object, that is to say of the enlivened finite creation with infinite or transcendent G-dliness, is a theme found with striking emphasis in one of the great figures of Chassidic thought, at the time of Hegel and the late Enlightenment, Rabbi Schneur Zalman of Liadi. The dimension of G-dliness which unifies finite G-dliness (creation) and transcendent G-dliness, is a level of G-dliness *which* is higher than both of these. This level in G-dliness, which

---

[17] Talmud Tractate *B'rochos* 10a.
[18] See chapter 3 on the sense of immanent G-dliness, which has a transcendent root and quality even in its enclothement within the creation.

originates and coordinates the transcendent and immanent or delimiting G-dly "powers", is called *Atzmus*, literally "Quintessentiality". Whilst immanent G-dliness can be *positively* comprehended as the specific, indwelling *animus* of each entity, and transcendent G-dliness can be *negatively* comprehended as the engendering principle which is *beyond* description, *Atzmus*, quintessential or absolute G-dliness, in the words of Rabbi Sholom Dov Ber Schneersohn, is the negation of the positive and negation of negation: it is the *absolutely* transcendent[19]. It is G-dliness as Creator, as Master of the process or act of creation, which employs both transcendent and immanent, delimiting powers of G-dliness; just as in a profane sense, Hegel was to speak of the "Absolute" as the principle of *all* there is, which unites, and contains within itself the dialectic of, subject and object.

The modern - post-Hegelian - philosophy of the *individual*, in both secular and Jewish forms, however, touches the very question of the *agency* of this working of the unity of subject and object, immanent and transcendent. Just as the contemporary philosophy of the individual in Adorno sought to find in the individual the locus of a redemptive reconciliation of subject and object, man and the "second nature" of the technologically organized world, so do we find an analogous and yet utterly different phenomenon in Judaism. In the philosophies of Rabbi Menachem Mendel Schneerson and Rabbi Joseph B. Soloveitchik we see how the individual expresses - indeed serves as the agency - of Quintessential G-dliness, *Atzmus*, in reconstituting creation such as to house within it transcendent G-dliness. The pivotal significance of the individual Jew is the expression of the fact that he or she participates in *Atzmus*, which alone has the power to wed creation and transcendent G-dliness.

---

[19] *Sefer Ma'amarim 5666* (N.Y., Kehos), p. 168.

Let us now proceed to closer studies of Maimonides, the Maharal of Prague, Rabbi Schneur Zalman of Liadi and Rabbi Menachem Mendel Schneerson and Rabbi J.B. Soloveitchik in the epochs, which they characteristically but distinctively share with general thought.

CHAPTER 2

APPREHENDING THE TRANSCENDENT
MAIMONIDES AND MEDIEVAL PHILOSOPHY

The common feature of Maimonides' and medieval thought (here exemplified by Augustine and Aquinas) is that it gives priority to an objective - Divinely governed - reality. The subject, the human mind, seeks to apprehend this order, which it acknowledges as encompassing and transcending it. Yet there is a radical difference between the ways Maimonides, on the one hand, and Augustine and Aquinas, on the other apprehend this transcendence.

The comparison is elaborated in relation to three issues: (i) How are the multiple, determinate phenomena of creation to be understood in relation to their foundation, the transcendently one Creator; (ii) What is the relationship to reason of the Divinely ordained notions of the good? (iii) How does Divine Providence relate to subjective human will?

In each of these questions we find Maimonides driven to a notion of the radical transcendence of G-d. This affords, at best, a negative resolution of these questions. For Augustine and Aquinas, the transcendent tends to be conflated, or to use Adorno's term, identified, with intellectual, philosophical categories.

1. G-d and creation

The medieval philosophical setting

The difference between classical and medieval thought, is expressed by the historian of philosophy Frederick Copleston[1] in the following terms. Classical - Greek and Roman - thought was interested in the "how" of reality; the medieval philosophers were concerned with the phenomenon "that" it exists. For Plato and Aristotle, there was no question but that there is an objective order of reality guided by certain principles. All that was required for them was to describe these. The same applies in the Jewish epoch contemporaneous with classical Western thought. The sages of the Mishnah and the Talmud were people of great attachment and closeness to G-d. The existence of G-d and His unity, as reflected in creation, did not require any demonstration or reflection. Both they and their gentile counterparts lived - in Hegelian terms - in a relation of *immediacy* to the notion of a total, ordered objective reality.

The character of medieval thought, on the other hand, represents in Jewish terms a decline of the generations (in Maimonides' words, "a lessening of hearts [that is: minds]"[2]), so that knowledge becomes an issue of belief, and to believe becomes an issue. Hegel puts it that the relationship or attitude of *belief* in medieval theology expresses an interruption to the immediacy of understanding of the sense of wholeness of reality, and of the Principle behind the Whole. Henceforth, there is the believing individual *and* that which he or she

---

[1] F. Copleston, *A History of Philosophy*, Vol. 3 Part II N.Y.: Doubleday (Image books), 1963, p. 242. This statement is made particularly in connection with the relationship of Aquinas and Aristotle. See also *A History of Philosophy*, Vol. 2, Part II, pp. 26-27.

[2] Introduction to the *Mishneh Torah*.

believes. The term "belief" expresses a commitment to that construed reality. What was simply known now requires a reflection upon that knowledge. That is, the knowledge of reality must become *foundational*: it must seek the foundation of being - *why* and *that* things are and not only *how* they are. Moreover, the *that* becomes the reciprocal condition of the *how*: the analysis of reality is directly related to the understanding of its foundation, G-d.

The synthesis of the perspective of a total *objective* reality, carried on from classical thought, and the more reflective and foundational quality of medieval philosophy is achieved through the mediation of objective reality by categories of mind. In Adorno and Horkheimer's words[3], medieval thought is *metaphysical* as distinct from the mythological or cosmological character of Greek and Roman thought. It uses categories of mind, discusses principles and results of mental knowing, but it ascribes these results to the objective reality itself, rather than treating them simply as the lens of the human mind. The mind is not a stranger to reality, which it tackles *experimentally*, as Francis Bacon was to make it. Philosophical, mental categories are directly attributed to the object. Thought does not think about its own subjective limitation or predicament: it goes directly to a higher or truer reality - *meta*physics.

The fact that medieval thought traces back the existence and nature of reality to a Creator, means that the major categories of thought - in terms of Hegel's *Logic*, "being", "essence", "process" - are themselves connected with *theology*. *Being* will be linked with creation, or G-d as Creator, *Essence* will be associated with Divinely communicated good and *Process* will be associated with a notion of providence. Since, in other

---

[3] As presented in the first section of chapter 1 of this monograph.

words, reality is *founded* upon G-d, medieval thought must seek to "understand" G-d, in order to comprehend reality, which by definition is *creation*. Thus, to begin with the nature of being itself, medieval metaphysics addresses the questions of the "existence" or "being" of G-d. This in turn relates to the question of the "attributes" of G-d. Specifically, if the creation is founded on a Creator, it must necessarily reflect the unity of the Creator. Plurality, particularity and particularly the discordance of evil in creation thus become an issue, posing a contradiction to the unity of the Creator. A theological metaphysics requires a resolution of the unity of the Creator with the multiplicity of the Creation. In this, as in other areas of medieval theology and metaphysics, there are two signal approaches. One works in the neo-Platonist mould as exemplified by Augustine and the other in a neo-Aristotelian way as found in Aquinas.

In relation to the neo-Platonist background of Augustine, Copleston writes:

Plato had maintained a doctrine of archetypal ideas or essences, and whatever Plato himself may or may not have thought, the neo-Platonists at least 'located' these ideas in the divine mind, so that... Augustine was enabled to praise Plato and Plotinus on this account[4].

In the Christian context of Augustine, however, neo-Platonism had further to be given a creationist character: forms, instead of being hypostasized as reality, became "divine ideas", from which reality was *created*. This became the doctrine of "exemplarism" fully developed in the later middle ages by Bonaventure. In Copleston's words (which I quote

---

[4] *A History of Philosophy*, Vol. 2, Part I, p. 289. See *The City of G-d* (transl. M. Dods, G. Wilso, J.J. Smith in Whitney J. Oates (Ed) *Basic Writings of St. Augustine*, N.Y: Random House, 1948), VIII, 5.

since the original works of Augustine here cited by Copleston are presently inaccessible to me):

> The species of created things have their ideas or *rationes* in G-d, and G-d from all eternity saw in Himself, as possible reflections of Himself, the things which He could create and would create. He knew them before creation as they are in Him, as Exemplar, but He made them as they exist, i.e. as external and finite reflections of His divine essence[5].

G-d thus becomes the projector, the antecedent Idea of creation - the *apriori* of all being - which despite the creationism of Augustine, makes G-d nevertheless in a sense *continuous* with the creation. In *idea*, the particulars of creation already *inhere* in the Creator. In the neo-Platonist cast of Augustine's thought, G-d is the "highest" and "unchangeable" good from which all good things, spiritual and physical come. Bad in the creation, on the other hand, is to be understood as a *corruption* or *privation* of the good. As Augustine argues in many places - his principal animus being against the Manichaeans - evil is not a substance, a reality, but simply a privation of the good. From the best things to the worst, we find a better reflection to that which is judged as not being a reflection of G-d. In other words only those things which possess "good measure, form or order" could be said to reflect G-d[6]. Thus, whilst Augustine maintains a transcendental creationist principle - an unchangeable God - this finds its reflection, and thus in a sense definition, in the perfection of creation, for which it serves as Exemplar. G-d becomes, the first principle, the *a priori* of the entire creation, comprehended

---

[5] *A History of Philosophy*, Vol. 2, Part I, p. 87.

[6] Augustine, "Concerning the Nature of the Good" (in *Basic Writings of St. Augustine*), chs 1-6.

as a hierarchy from goodness through its corruption into evil[7].

Aquinas, on the other hand, being the empirical neo-Aristotelian, who works back from the observation of material reality to the concept of G-d, a *posteriori*, achieves the unity of the infinite and the particular quite differently. For him knowledge of the Divine is so to speak the ultimately perfect *extrapolation* from the finite: the perfection of - *proceeding from* - all perfections. In Copleston's words,

> . . . to say that G-d is *ipsum esse* ["existence itself", which is Aquinas' positive determination of G-d's essence] is to give, as it were, His inner nature . . . Every other name is in some way inadequate . . . the statement that G-d is infinite Justice is an inadequate expression of the Divine essence. The names we employ in speaking of G-d are derived from an experience of determinate forms and express primarily those forms; but the name, *He who is* signifies not a determinate form, but 'the infinite ocean of substance'[8].

That is, G-d is the ultimate substratum of being, the most simple and all-encompassing predicate, namely "being" itself, "the infinite ocean of substance", and this is achieved as a "regress", though it is not properly grasped, from more specific and determinate forms. Consequently, the oneness of G-d "resides" within detail, so that all contradiction between the oneness of His being, and the multiplicity of creation, is removed by calling Him "being itself". This being is the mover

---

[7] Aquinas attacks the error of Augustine in affirming G-d as the "world-soul" *Summa Theologica* I, Q.3, viii. An editor of the *Summa Theologica*, A.C.Pegis (in the edition *Basic Writings of St. Thomas Aquinas*, N.Y: Random House, 1944) cites as the reference for Aquinas' statement, Augustine's *The City of G-d*, VII, 6.

[8] *A History of Philosophy*, Vol. 2, Part II, p. 81. "Substance" is here to be understood in the sense of "being" (see references in subsequent fn.).

and spirit of all things, but in Aquinas' doctrine, it remains forever distinct from - not taking on - the essence of the things of which it is mover and spirit. At one and the same time, Aquinas maintains a theistic position, that G-d is not defined by the essences of the Creation which are added to their being, and yet the most fundamental predicate of Creation, being itself, is shared by G-d and the creation[9].

By an opposite path, Aquinas has come to the same result as Augustine. Where Augustine found a continuity between the infinite or the Absolute and the finite creation by comprehending G-d as the *presumptive and projective* first principle, Aquinas *derives* G-d as the ultimate principle, of the *creation itself.*

Maimonides and Divine transcendence

In Maimonides we encounter something radically different. The notion of Augustine that the creation is a reflection of the "divine mind", which is its "Exemplar" is excluded by Maimonides' notion of the unity of G-d, as set down in his commentary on the Mishnah as one of the thirteen principles of faith, which states:

> . . . [G-d's] unity is not like that of a kind or a species [a division of a kind], nor like one thing compounded which can be broken into many [qualitative] components, nor [is He] one in the sense of a simple body, which is a [qualitative] unit but can be infinitely divided and differentiated. Rather, He, be He exalted, is a unity, which does not find its likeness in any respect . . . [10]

---

[9] See *Summa Theologica* I,Q.3, vii, viii; Q.8, ii.

[10] Tractate *Sanhedrin*, chapter 10. The translation is that of the present writer.

In this statement Maimonides proceeds from the most obviously compounded unities to the simplest unities in the creation. The species is the abstract unifying characteristic of a variety of palpably distinct and independent individuals. This unity is no more than a likeness. A body compounded of different parts represents a higher degree of unity, the different parts actually cohere and partake in one common existence. Still this likeness can be differentiated into component parts with distinct identities. Its unity is then exceeded by that of a simple body, that is one qualitative substance, which is however quantitatively divisible. The creation ostensibly knows of no simpler - that is, more intensely unified - unity, than a simple substance which possesses spatial extension. And yet this is not an example for the unity of G-d. In other words, where Augustine will seek to reduce all the ideas of G-d to one idea, from which all ideas pertaining to the creation emerge, for Maimonides this could not define the "divine Mind" or the "divine Essence". For G-d does not correspond to the creation as its Exemplar, its most ineffable "model". This will come out even more concretely in Maimonides' notion of the "Knowledge" of G-d.

The point of this is that the unity of G-d does not need to be measured against the creation, since G-d's existence is not in the plane of the existence of creation. And Maimonides' progressive negation of the different kinds of unity exhibited by material creation comes to demonstrate not only that G-d's unity is transcendent of the creation, but conceivably also to suggest that any attempt to make sense of G-d from the order of creation, or vice versa, is to mistake the transcendent nature of G-d. There is no "problem" for the unity of G-d in the concrete multiplicity of the creation, for they exist on a different plane. G-d transcends the creation *absolutely* and yet is "involved" in its creation. There is no need for a rational or philosophical accommodation of finite existence *with* the infinite existence of G-d. For G-d can *relate* to the creation, as its Creator, and yet, as we shall see, be the negation of its properties.

A similar point arises in relation to Aquinas' characterization of G-d as "existence itself", that is as the ultimate substratum - though not in a pantheistic, but rather theist or creationist sense - in which the being of the creation participates. It is simply that according to Aquinas, G-d's existence and essence are the same: His essence is being, whilst all created beings have a superimposed essence, or accidental quality. Maimonides, however, states in the first of the thirteen principles:

> . . . there is an existent being, perfect in every manner of existence, and He is the cause of the existence of all existent beings. In Him is the maintenance of their existence, and from Him they draw their existence. If one could picture the absence of His existence, then the existence of all things would be nullified, and they would not remain in existence. But if [on the other hand] there could be pictured the absence of the existence of all beings apart from Him, then His existence, be He exalted, would not be nullified nor would it be lacking anything. For He, be He exalted, does not need anything else for His existence; whereas everything else, from the spiritual intelligences, that is the angels and the bodies of the spheres, and that which is below them, require Him for their existence.[11]

Here is a notion that G-d exists - indeed the first of Maimonides' principles is that G-d exists - but it is not an existence on the plane of the creation itself. Aquinas abstracts G-d as the being *from which the being of the* creation derives, albeit different from anything else in creation (simply 'being'

---

[11] Commentary on the Mishnah, *Sanhedrin*, ch. 10.

itself). Maimonides' notion of the existence of G-d, is of a radically transcendent existence, *which is in no way tied* to the existence of the creation. It is simply the *cause* of the being of the creation, and the creation in no way acquires G-d's being. Thus it is explained by Maimonides in the *Moreh N'vuchim* (the *Guide for the Perplexed*),[12] as we shall presently see, that if we affix to G-d the attribute of "existing" it is not in the sense of any notion of "existence" which the Creation possesses.

Since this is so, there would seem to be a problem from the various descriptions or "attributes" ("knowing", "merciful" and so forth) ascribed to G-d, which clearly make sense in terms of, and relate to, phenomena of the creation. For if G-d transcends the creation, how could any description be applied to him? And yet revealed Scripture does use names such as "merciful" and "knowing" in relation to G-d. Maimonides doctrine of the attributes of G-d responds to this issue. In general, Maimonides states in the *Guide* there are two kinds of attributes, which can meaningfully be applied to G-d. One kind of attributes, such as those connoting kindness and severity or mercy, relate to G-d's *actions* in the framework of the creation. Thus G-d, in fashioning a creation - which could also have been a very different one from that which exists - made a world which comprehends kindness, mercy and so forth, so that these attributes are patently directed towards the world and are for the sake of the world. In short they describe only actions meaningful for the creation, and there is no logical difficulty in the idea that these do not, and need not, inhere in G-d.[13] These are external and extrinsic qualities, and there is no contradiction to the sense of G-d as being utterly transcendent of any characteristic of the creation. The issue arises in relation to those attributes which do not patently relate to actions of

---

[12] Part I, ch. 67.
[13] *Ibid.*, Part I, chs 53-54.

G-d, but to "Himself", such as "existing", "knowing", "powerful", "living", and "willing", but represent "essential" or "intrinsic" qualities. We cannot solve this question by saying that they refer to "external actions".

Maimonides states in relations to these attributes, that they can only be applied *negatively*. That is to say, we cannot say that G-d does not know, does not live, is not powerful, does not will; but we cannot state them in a positive way and with this be content that we have made a positive description of G-d in relation to them. In two places in the *Mishneh Torah*[15] Maimonides does elaborate on one of these attributes - "knowledge" - from which we can learn to the others

. . . [G-d] does not know with a knowledge which is external to Himself as we do. For we and our knowledge are not one and same thing. But as for the Creator, be He blessed, He and His knowledge and His life are one in every way and respect and every manner of unity . . . One may therefore say that He is the Knower, He is the Known and He is the Knowledge itself - all one. And the mouth has no power to explain this, nor the ear to comprehend it, nor the mind of man to grasp it clearly.[16]

When we say that G-d "knows", His knowledge is not like anything we associate with this term. For in earthly terms, if I know something, there is I, the knower, the object (say, a flower) which is the known and the knowledge of this flower which is a new piece of knowledge, which in turn could impact upon me. There is in other words a causal interaction of distinct elements. G-d's knowledge of something, however, as explained in Chassidic thought[17], is simultaneously its

---

[14] *Ibid.*, Part I, ch. 66.
[15] *Hilchos Y'sodei HaTorah* 2:10, *Hilchos T'shuvah* 5:5.
[16] *Hilchos Y'sodei HaTorah* 2:10. Present author's translation.
[17] *Tanya (Likkutei Amarim)*, ch. 42.

enlivening and He knows it inasmuch as He knows Himself, Who brings it into, and holds it in, existence. The being thing is in no way separate from G-dliness, but is rather encompassed and pervaded by It.[18] Its existence, and consequently the knowledge of its existence is "spontaneous": there operates no causality, no transitions from potentiality to actuality.[19] There is no separation of elements - G-d, the known object, and the knowledge - in relation to which the interactions described above on an earthly plane could exist. Only "below", do things become separate from G-d so to speak, from *their* point of view. In short, there operates a transcendent logic which we can adumbrate only negatively, as indeed the prophet did, when he said - and Maimonides adduces his words, in discussing this point : "My thoughts are not your thoughts , nor are your ways my ways".[20]

Accordingly, when a transcendent G-d enclothes Himself in an attribute which the creation understands, such as "knowledge", it demonstrates a transcendent and unlimited - a *negative* - manifestation of that attribute. Based on this the *Tzemach Tzedek* went on to say, that this is true of all the attributes of G-d, even those which relate to external actions. A transcendent G-d thus manifests a transcendent "kindness" and a transcendent "mercy".[21] At all events, for Maimonides the transcendence of G-d is a rigorous one: there is no continuity whatsoever between it and the categories of creation or created intellect.

---

[18] *Ibid.*, ch. 48.

[19] See Rabbi Sholom Dovber of Lubavitch, *Sefer Ma'amarim* 5644 (N.Y: Kehos, 1982), p. 205.

[20] In *Hilchos T'shuvah* 5:5, quoting *Isaiah* 55:8.

[21] See Rabbi Menachem Mendel of Lubavitch *(Tzemach Tzedek)*, *Or HaTorah, parshas Vayero*, p. 1530f. (cited in *Sefer HaLikkutim* of the *Tzemach Tzedek* [N.Y: Kehos, 1982], s.v. *"Hu Hayodei'a"*)

2. Reason and revelation

Natural law

The concept of a transcendent good is the root notion of the medieval concept of "natural law. It stands in opposition to "positive law" in the sense of law *constituted* by humans, whether by the sovereign or by other elements - including the legislature - of a society. It is not law which finds a criterion in the conditions of its human origination, but rather *its* conditions precede and arbitrate the rightness of any humanly originated law. An absolute notion of "justice" precedes law.

The source of natural law - in the words of Aquinas, who brings medieval natural law doctrines to their classic formulation - is reason, "instilled by G-d"[22] in the mind of man, which only an extraneous human perversity *can obscure*. Natural law proceeds from this reason, which produces a transcendent law encompassing *all* humanity at all times: for this law establishes, to use Aquinas's words, the "rule and measure"[23] of things.

The concept of the priority and supremacy of natural law in relation to human laws was already stated quite baldly in the words of Augustine:

Justice being taken away [i.e. without prior reference to a natural standard of justice], then, what are Kingdoms but great robberies? For what are robberies themselves, but little Kingdoms. The band itself is made up of man; it is ruled by the authority of a prince, it is knit together by the pact of confederacy; the booty is divided by the law agreed upon.[24]

---

[22] *Summa Theologica*, XIII, Q. 90, iv.; Q. 93, ii.
[23] *Ibid.*, XIII, Q. 90, ii.
[24] City of G-d, 4,4.

Copleston puts it as follows: "the State will not embody true justice, will not be a really moral State, unless it is a Christian state: it is Christianity which makes men good citizens . . . the Church must permeate the State by her principles . . . [So it is that] Augustine stands at the head of the medieval exaltation of the Church vis-à-vis the State . . .".[25] In Aquinas' formulation, there is apart from natural law - deriving from the "eternal law, existing in G-d", a divine wisdom which must ultimately guide human conduct - also a faculty of *human* law. Human law, however, "has the nature of law insofar as it partakes of right reason; and it is clear that in this respect it is derived from eternal law".[26] It is not that there is no sense of the State or society in Aquinas, but society is subordinate to the natural law.

Natural law, as eternal and prior and universal, is immutable and where there are changes, this is explained in the following terms:

> . . . natural law is the same for all . . . the natural law is altogether unchangeable in its first principles. But in its secondary principles which . . . are certain detailed proximate conclusions . . . it may be changed in some particular cases of rare occurrence . . ."[27]

Copleston explains it thus: Aquinas'

> . . . admission of the changeability of the secondary precepts of the natural law in particular cases refers rather to what the Scholastics called a *mutatio materiae* than to a change in the precept itself: it is rather that circumstances of the act are so

---

[25] *A History of Philosophy*, Vol. 2 Pt I, p.104

[26] *Summa Theologica* XIII, Q. 93, iii. See also M.P. Golding (Ed.), *The Nature of Law* (N.Y: Random House, 1966) which anthologizes passages from Aquinas, together with articles of commentary and critique.

[27] *Summa Theologica* XIII, Q. 94, ii, iv, v.

changed that it no longer falls under the prohibition than that the prohibition itself is changed.[28]

Here is not the place to go into this doctrine of the immutability of the natural law. In short, the natural law has the claims of a transcendent law, namely that it is universal and prior to any particular time or place and that it is immutable. We shall later return to the claim of natural law to be implanted in "divinely instilled" *reason*.

Maimonides: the character of revelation

Similar to "natural law" we find in Torah the concept of halachah or law as preceding any recipient or practitioner of that law. In the words of the early major work of Jewish mysticism, the *Zohar*, which we quoted in the previous chapter, "the Holy One, blessed be He, looked into the Torah and created the world". Torah as the body of doctrine setting forth the six hundred and thirteen commandments (*mitzvos*), originates in the level of Divine *will*, which is "simple" - transcendently superior - in relation to "understanding".[30] If the commandments can also be explicated on the plane of intellect, which Maimonides claims they can be and are at length explained in the *Guide of the Perplexed*, nevertheless the *source* of the mitzvos is not reason. Their having been *given*, it is desirable to exercise understanding to appreciate the functions of the mitzvos[31], but that cannot take us to the source and ultimate "reason" of mitzvos.

---

[28] *Op. cit.* p. 128.

[29] *Zohar*, Part 2, 161b.

[30] See *Likkutei Sichos*, Vol. 13 p.66ff.

[31] See *Guide*, part III, chapter 31.

So it is that Maimonides explains the foundation of the laws, precepts, of the Torah as *revelation*.[32] As a writer on Maimonides has stated, the foundation of the mitzvos is essentially non-cognitive[33] and that it is prophecy, a supra-philosophical activity, which alone affords access to that *metaphysical* realm of first truths and primary goods. Indeed, it has been pointed out that reason itself leads to the acknowledgment that the first principles and ground norms of moral theory are *beyond* intellect.[34] The criterion which Maimonides sets out for the invalidation of an otherwise "accredited" prophet is that the prophet prophesies to add or subtract on a permanent basis a mitzva of the Torah. This shows his prophecy to be false inasmuch as it contradicts the Torah (containing the six hundred and thirteen mitzvos) given to Moses. And the validity of the Torah given by Moses is not a consequence of wonders he performed, but because the Jewish people themselves participated in the *suprarational* experience of revelation of Sinai, where they witnessed the communication of G-d with Moses. This was an experience

---

[32] *Hilchos Y'sodei HaTorah*, chapters 7-8.

[33] See Marvin Fox, *Interpreting Maimonides - Studies in Methodology, Metaphysics and Moral Philosophy*, Chicago: University of Chicago Press, 1990, p. xi *et passim*. Fox argues for a "dialectical tension" between rationalist and suprarationalist perspectives in the *Guide* of Maimonides. We would prefer to explain this, as above, in the first section of this chapter, that a transcendent G-dliness enclothes itself in the creation, including the created intellect, and the resultant negative formulations of intellect are then a *necessary* result of this *enclothement*. Professor Fox presents this as an intellectually honestly experienced "tension" by Maimonides who wishes to approach these issues from the *two equal* perspectives of philosophical neutrality and religious commitment. Rather, we would argue, the *prior* stance is religious commitment, which *then* enters the realm of intellect, as far as - and in the negative manner in which - intellect permits.

[34] See *Likkutei Sichos*, Vol. 2, pp. 561-62.

given to the spiritual transhistorical "we" -the souls - of the Jewish people.[35]

Maimonides and the natural law tradition, as shared by Augustine but epitomized by Aquinas, have in common that they both present what is claimed to be a transcendent, objective law which is eternal and prior to any constitutive body, including the state - a notion of *morality* which directs and adjudicates the rightness of human conduct in all circumstances. The difference between Maimonides and Aquinas is that Aquinas roots this in human *reason*; whilst for Maimonides it *essentially* transcends reason: it begins on a plane above reason, and whilst reason can subsequently analyze, it cannot derive or establish, it.

With this the criticism applied to natural law cannot be applied to Maimonides. The criticism raised against natural law is : "whose reason?" - where does this reason, supposedly instilled in mankind by G-d, finds its definition?[36] Where, in other words, a particular law is asserted as "natural" and accessed by "reason", it founders on a secret positivity (having been originated by a particular intellect or group of persons) which is hypostazied as a Divine law. In summary, by locating the divine law in reason it has in fact conflated the transcendent law with particular *human* reason. Revelation, in the teaching of Maimonides, on the other hand, acknowledges the law which has been given from *beyond reason*.

---

[35] See *Hilchos Y'sodei HaTorah* 8:3.

[36] See A. Ross, "A critique of the philosophy of natural law", in M.P. Golding, *op. cit.*, pp.71-2.

3. Providence and human will

Augustine and Aquinas

One of the issues in which the difference between medieval non-Jewish (specifically Christian) and Jewish thought comes out most strikingly is in the issue of free choice and Divine knowledge. This emerges elsewhere as the issue of freedom and Divine providence or control of the direction of history. For certainly the medieval Christian view, held with Jewish thought, that there is a Divine supervision in history. In Copleston's words:

> To the Christian history is necessarily of profound importance. It was in history that man fell, in history that he was redeemed: it is in history, progressively, that the [. . . church] grows and develops and that G-d's plan is unfolded.[37]

Now it is patent that if human choice is posited, the sense in which G-d's will is necessarily unfolded is at the least paradoxical. For if the actual choices of humans are known in advance, then how could these choices be said to be free? And conversely, if the upshot of human choices were truly indeterminate, then how could we posit an objective Divine providence in history functioning independent of man?

The resolution of this problem, given by Augustine is that the Divine law, which has been *instilled* in human nature, similarly impels the will towards the good. Just as evil is a privation or a corruption of the good, so too the turning of the will away from G-d, is a "privation of right order in the created will"[38], the inherent will of man towards the divinely ordained good.

---

[37] *A History of Philosophy*, Vol. 2, Part I, pp. 100-101. See here also the *Enchridion* chs. 11-13 in *Basic Works of St. Augustine, op. cit.*
[38] *Ibid.*, p.100.

Thus, notwithstanding potential *degeneration*, the concrete individual, in the full facticity of his power of choice is generally *impelled* by his nature towards the good.

Copleston adduces from various places in the writings of Aquinas that the will of man is, in a way similar to that argued by Augustine, impelled by its nature to the divine good so that he sees "man in the *concrete*, as called to a supernatural end"[39]:

> The will necessarily desires happiness, beatitude, and de facto this beatitude can be found only in the vision of G-d: we can say, therefore, that the concrete human being necessarily desires the vision of G-d.[40]

The result is similar to our discussion in the last section. There is a conflation, to the one plane, of human nature and will with the Divine law operating in reality. There is the purported transcendence of the Divine law, in which case we would paradoxically be forced to say that man has been or is elevated to the level of the Divine. Or alternatively, this can only mean that the conception of the Divine will has been tailored to a human scale: a secret positivity functions in the notion of the Divine itself, a coalescence of the human and the Divine; and as such it is open to the ridicule of simple empirical and historical observation.

In summary, in the metaphysics of Augustine and Aquinas, the Divine law is implanted in human nature. Man *wants* what G-d wants. Nature merges with the supernatural. Here a transcendent view is glimpsed: *G-d's* plan is worked out; but this is *through* human reason, which is its organon. Subject reveals in its own terms the great Object which works through it. In fact the conflation of human reason with providence and the Divine intention and "law" corresponds very closely to

---

[39] *A History of Philosophy*, Vol. 2, part II, p.122; emphasis added.
[40] *Ibid.*, p. 123.

Adorno's picture of the actual, concrete subjectivity at work in medieval "objectivist" philosophy". Object - G-dliness- is primary and central, but it is disclosed through the subject, human intellect and reason, and in reality it *is* subjective, *human* reason.

Maimonides

For Maimonides freedom of choice is an empirical reality and a major premise of the Torah[41], for it would have been absurd to give precepts - *imperatives* (mitzvos) - to human beings without choice, without the ability to chose good *and* bad, robots which can do none other than what they have been "programmed" to do. And, moreover, the entire system of reward and punishment is meaningless without choice, for if a person is *impelled* by inner or outer nature to do something, why should he be rewarded or punished on account of it.

At the same time there is an equal principle that there is nothing outside the jurisdiction of G-d, namely, there is no enclave of creation which is not directed and sustained by G-d in its existence, inasmuch as the creation reflects the *unity* of its Creator. To deny the absolute sovereignty and "ownership" of G-d in His creation, would be tantamount to denying His unity, namely that there is nothing "outside", no lacuna in which His constant creative and sustaining power and hence dominion does not operate. There is no delimitation of the dominion of G-d. In the words of Maimonides, nothing "can be done in the world without the permission of man's Owner and without His will"[42]. From this follows an obvious paradox. Entailed in G-d's unity is, as Maimonides states, His omniscience. This includes His knowing what is going to be even before it takes place and this relates also to the upshot of

---

[41] *Hilchos T'shuvah* ch. 5.
[42] *Ibid.*, 5:6.

moral choices. Now if G-d knows that a person will chose such and such, how is it possible that the person will not make that choice? And if, on the other hand, a person is assured real freedom of choice, what becomes of G-d's omniscience and jurisdiction? The fact is, however, that both axiomatic principles are simultaneously valid: G-d knows what will be and yet freedom of choice is given to mankind. Here is a logical contradiction or paradox. But it is a contradiction or paradox only for *created intellect*.

A resolution of this paradox is presented in the commentary, *Medrash Shmuel*, on the tractate *Ethics of the Fathers*.[43] Since G-d is *above time* altogether (past, present and future all being equal before Him) His knowledge of the outcome of the free choice of a person in the future is possible because, being above time, it as though for G-d the choice *has already taken place*. Consequently, G-d's knowledge proceeds from the choice and we can explain this as a *causality* between the results of free choice and G-d's knowledge.

Yet Maimonides does not even seek an explanation of this kind, but states that the nature of Divine omniscience is *beyond* human understanding altogether. Nowhere does Maimonides' radically transcendent perspective come out more patently than in his treatment of the issue of Divine providence and human choice. When, as noted before, Maimonides says that G-d is the Knower, the Knowledge and the Known, this means that G-d's knowledge is of a special nature - outside natural relationships and causalities. In the words of the Lubavitcher Rebbe, the explanation of the *Medrash Shmuel* works at the level where G-d's knowledge has been "contracted" into natural-intellectual terms. It is not wrong, but its *logic* is "earthly": it functions in the categories

---

[43] In the name of Rabbi M. Almosninu; cited in *Likkutei Sichos*, Vol. 27, p. 252, fn. 14.

of created intellect. Maimonides is speaking from the Divine perspective, that is to say, from the level of *transcendent* G-dliness in which "knowledge" as applied to G-d has a transcendent form, one which negates the ordinary categories of intellect. When "knowledge" or "knowing" is applied to a transcendent G-dliness it becomes different, other. As explained above with regard to Maimonides in relation to the attributes of G-d: this ispasses and transcends human logic. It can be intimated through reason, but as the transcendence of reason logic: both logics function. Both perspectives exist, but Maimonides' *primary focus* is on the transcendent "logic" of Divine knowledge.

Whereas for Augustine and Aquinas there is a conflation of subject - natural intellect with its categories - with the objective G-dliness, for Maimonides the transcendent perspective of G-dliness is preserved in its full rigour. The theological definition of transcendent G-dliness in Jewish thought is "that it participates in creation but creation does not participate in it". Human intellect, *philosophical* reason is *part* of creation, so that in no way could the categories or predicates of reason be applied to transcendental G-dliness. If - and as indeed - reason *does* relate to G-dliness at this level, this is through its own *negation*. Transcendent G-dliness possesses a logic which *encompasses* and *transcends* human logic. It can be intimated through reason, but as the transcendence of reason.

CHAPTER 3

THE LOGIC OF IMMANENCE
THE MAHARAL OF PRAGUE
AND THE RENAISSANCE

This chapter explores the common shift of focus, in both general and Jewish thought from an objective, metaphysical reality transcending the subject, to the centrality of the subject within (immanent to) reality. For Francis Bacon, this meant making the human mind the conscious arbitrator of meaning and useful knowledge of reality. In the Jewish philosophy of the Maharal of Prague, it relates to a change of emphasis from the perspective of transcendent G-dliness *to that of G-dliness, housed immanently within the Creation, which is associated with a subject within Creation: the Jewish people. Mystical philosophy here refers to the Shechina, the* indwelling Presence *of the transcendent G-d, and to the Jewish people as vehicle or "limbs" of the* Shechina.

The ethical dimension of the Renaissance philosophy of Niccolo Machiavelli is expressed as a moral principle of the vigour and vitality of the subject: here the leader of the sovereign state, as against the so-conceived tyranny of the supratemporal and universal authority of the Catholic church. For the Maharal, on the other hand, the moral sovereignty and integrity of the Jewish people relates to its spiritual "form", which has its perfection and force only when it is connected with the transcendent Torah. For this is the sense of the Jewish people: a transcendent "form" drawn within the creation.

Having secularized a theological or metaphysical notion of creation as "nature", Renaissance thought - in the form of Shakespearean tragedy - inserts the subject into nature as its "head". Nature becomes a reflex of man: it is flawed humanity *which produces a cathartic convulsion in nature. The disorder of creation as a whole for the Maharal, however, is the result of the* spiritual malaise and disunity *of the Jewish people. When the Jewish people are whole and united in their proper place, this is the redemption not only of the Jewish people, but of Creation as a whole.*

1. Subject and sovereignty

The assertion of the subject

Even though the Renaissance, as the word ("rebirth") seems to suggest, may have sought foundations in a supposedly classical model of man, it was in fact an unprecedentedly new phenomenon. It represents the rejection of a universal or total order of reality, an *objective* - in medieval terms, Divine - order, *into* which man simply fits as *part* of the scheme of things. Although the notion of an encompassing objective reality in foregoing epochs had undergone various forms (as noted in the first chapter) - it always had the character of objectivity. The novelty and significance of the Renaissance in secular thought is quite simply the placing of *man* and *human* intellect as the measure of all things. It is the rejection of any pre-given order, of a theologically conceived, total objective reality into which man fits, and to the prior or "natural" truth of which human intellect has to assimilate itself. The authority, or at least the usefulness, of knowledge now exists solely in that it derives from the self-consciously knowing subject. Even its Christianity, the Protestantism of the Reformation, is a reformed, "humanized" Christianity which bespeaks the centrality of the believer as against the transmundane authority of the Church.

For Renaissance thought the relationship of the subject to reality is *immanent*; that is, man has adopted a wholly earthly perspective. Reality makes sense in the field of human experience - in the realm of *science*. Francis Bacon (1561-1626), though conceivably he may have not have been the greatest of philosophers, is yet the representative of all that is modern in the Renaissance in its empirical, scientific spirit[1]. Copleston writes:

> If the pre-Socratic philosophers discovered Nature, in the sense that they formed the idea of a cosmos or law-governed system, the Renaissance scientists discovered Nature in the sense that they developed the use of scientific method in the discovery of the ëlawsí which actually govern natural events.[2]

The key notion here is found in the words "actually govern natural events". The subject works on the plane of *actual nature*. The vision of science in Francis Bacon has this practical, material quality: it *anticipates* technology. In the terms of Adorno and Horkheimer's *Dialectic of the Enlightenment*, the picture of the world as a giant laboratory has here its germ. Knowledge is not be had by reference to a transcendent, objective given; rather, knowledge is to be gained on the level of the immanent experience - data and scientific investigation - of the subject.

For Francis Bacon the issue is that of the *dominion* of man over nature. And this is the task of science. In order to conquer nature one must obey it, know its laws. Now, as has been argued elsewhere, science *per* se is as much compatible with

---

[1] It should be noted, though here is not the place to argue the point, that science *per se* is not compatible *only* with the outlook of the Renaissance. There was science beforehand, and a religious perspective by no means excludes science. By "scientific" we refer here to an attitude towards, or a philosophy of, science, which could perhaps better be termed "scientistic", as is later brought out.

[2] *A History of Philosophy*, Vol. 3. Part II, p. 244.

[3] Francis Bacon, *Novum Organum* I, 4. In *The Physical and Metaphysical Works of Lord Bacon* (ed. Joseph Devey), London: George Bell and Sons, 1894, the translation is "nature is only subdued by submission, and that which in contemplative philosophy corresponds with the cause in practical science becomes the rule" (p. 383)

religion as with other outlooks. The question is only what science is and what is essentially non-scientific speculation. This cannot concern us here. The *philosophy* of science, however, is something else again - it is not science; and what interests us here is Bacon's philosophy of science. It would seem that for Bacon useful scientific knowledge has two essential characteristics. The first is that it is experimental. That is, there is no usefully admissible knowledge of a *metaphysical* or *theological kind*. These species of knowledge are essentially "sterile" in comparison to the concern of *physics* in a very broad sense which is concerned with finding "material" and "efficient" causes, as distinct from the "final causes" of metaphysical speculation.

The second feature of Bacons doctrine of knowledge or science is his presentation of it as *inductive*. This Bacon comes to contrapose to the syllogistic of Aristotle, which had previously dominated reasoning. Its method was primarily *deductive*, and the propositions which form its premises, are barely submitted to analysis. For if they were, it would be found that they could only be *inductively* gathered. That is to say, truth must be found, and the "invention" (in a non-pejorative sense) of truth, that is to say its discovery, can only proceed by induction. Thus, regarding Aristotelian notions of induction as purely "enumerative"[4], that is serving as descriptions of bodies of information, Bacon sets out by an *eliminative* method in the analysis of the relationships of data to find causal relationships, the stuff of scientific investigation.[5] Bacon's notion of induction differs from the later classical doctrine of David Hume, based on the notion of the projection of observed conjunctions of events. Its sense of induction is that of progressively abstract analyses of information - by

---

[4] See Anthony Quinton, *Francis Bacon*, Oxford: O.U.P., 1980, p. 82.
[5] *Ibid.*, p. 60.

means of various rules and procedures - to elicit causal relationships. Induction *abstracts* knowledge. Mind immerses itself in the data of nature, to approximate ever more exactly its truth.[6]

The Maharal of Prague

The great figure of Jewish philosophy at the time of the Renaissance is Rabbi Yehudah Arieh Loewe (c.1526-1609), the *Maharal* (an acrostic of his rabbinical title and name) of Prague. In his time there lived other great watershed figures of Jewish thought: in Kabalah, the *Ari zal,* and in Jewish law, Rabbi Yosef Caro, the author of the *Shulchon Oruch.* Yet apart from the fact that he was a giant in all fields of Torah scholarship as seen in the range of his work and concerns, from Talmudic *novellae* to the Kabalah[7], he made a great contribution which we can call *philosophical.* His thought differs from that of the great medieval figures of Jewish scholarship, the *Rishonim,* with Maimonides as their exemplar, in ways which strongly resemble the change between medieval and renaissance general thought.

Maimonides, as we have seen, presents the principles of Jewish belief primarily from the perspective of a transcendent G-d. His principles discuss the existence, unity, incorporeality and absolute priority of G-d. These principles lay down the basis of all being, and relate it to its absolute foundation - G-d. His principles speak of G-d as the Conferrer of prophecy, of the Torah of G-d, its sanctity and immutability: the ethical realm is one which resides with, and originates from, G-d.

---

[6] See the excellent presentation of Bacon's inductive method in Michel Malherbe, "Bacon's Method of Science" in M. Peltonen (ed), *The Cambridge Companion to Bacon,* Cambridge: C.U.P., 1996.

[7] In accordance with the practical teachings of which, he made the *Golem,* the animated man of clay, to protect the Jews of Prague.

Finally, in speaking of providence and redemption, the treatment is that of Divine Providence and administration of reward and punishment and of the Redemption through a human messenger of G-d, the Messiah, and the Resurrection of the dead to be worked by G-d. Whilst man possesses choice, the action and exercise of this choice is understood *within* the matrix of the Divine direction and order of things. In short, in Maimonides one finds that theology takes the focus upon the deeds of G-d, and how this is the systemic *context* for human action.

The key notion[8] in the thought of the Maharal is the *centrality* of the spiritual and physical body of the *Jewish people*. The affinity of the Maharal with the change brought about by the Renaissance is therefore that he has located a "subject" of history *within* the creation. From the perspective of the Jewish people, as a transhistorical subject, it is meaningful to say that when the ancestors of presently living Jews were freed from Egypt, so were they ("we"). The core or essential reality of the Jewish people is an indestructible and morally pure spiritual entity. At this level the body of the Jewish people is fundamentally intact. The merits or demerits of individuals represent an external and incidental phenomenon.[9] This is because the Jewish people is not a self-constituted body which has chosen to "elect" G-dliness as its principle. Rather, G-d has chosen the Jewish, forging a

---

[8] See the essay *"Hamabet ho'eloki al k'lal Yisroel b'mishnat haMaharal"* in the work, *Luz Ha'emunah*. The focus of the Maharal on the Jewish people is different to the nature of the attention given to the character of the Jewish people in the *medieval* Jewish work, the *Kusari* of Rabbi Yehudah HaLevi. There the Jewish people are seen as being particularly fitted to be associated with the Shechina which is understood, much in the sense of Maimonides, as a transcendent *Other*; whereas in the Maharal, the *Shechina* - as spiritual form - is associated with the Jewish people in an immanent way: it resides with them or they form an extension of it.

[9] See Maharal, *Netzach Yisroel*, ch. 11.

necessary bond with the Jewish people. The fitness of the Jewish people for their special relationship with the G-d is their assertion of the spiritual *form (tzura)* over physical *matter (chomer)* in their own lives. The splitting of the sea - associated by the Maharal with G-d's choosing, and the bonding of an essential connection with, the Jewish people - which occurred in the exodus from Egypt, symbolized this. The sea connotes materiality; its splitting represents the definitive predominance of form over matter.[10] The point here, however, is that, notwithstanding the G-dly election of the Jewish people and their "removed" association with a transcendent G-dliness, they are nevertheless a nation of human beings *in this world*. The actor is the *people* Israel on the plane of nature and history. Whilst the souls of the Jewish people relate to that which is beyond *(nivdal)*, they are enclothed within the bodies of Jewish people situated within creation. Thus the Jewish people are characterized by the Maharal in a recurring metaphor of the daughter of a king married to a prosperous commoner. However much her husband may try to please her, she can never be completely at home in his house, for she knows a qualitatively different existence.

The Jewish people relate to the totality of creation, so to speak, as the first station of G-dliness passed immanently into it: they are the central vitality of its existence. As this would be put by Rabbi Schneur Zalman of Liadi, the seventh generation descendent, son-after-son, from the Maharal, in his *Tanya*

> . . . the community of Israel, comprising 600,000 particular souls [which are in turn subdivided], is the [source of] life for the world as a whole . . . And each one of them contains and is related to the vitality of one part in 600,000 of the totality

---

[10] Maharal, *Tiferes Yisroel*, ch. 40. See chapter 4 below where other views locate this *choice* with the giving of the Torah at Sinai, for which the exodus and the splitting of the sea is an introduction.

of the world, which [part] depends on his vital soul for its elevation to G-d through its own[the soul's] elevation . . .[11]

This may project a little too much from a later philosophy onto the doctrine of the Maharal. The theme of *refinement* and *transformation* of the creation by the Jewish people is not emphasized in the Maharal. What does emerge from his writings is the sense in which the Jewish people represent the spiritual within the creation. Since this spirituality *derives* from a transcendent source, a source beyond and wholly independent of creation, it naturally implies its dominion over transient materiality. And whilst this spirituality may be temporally submerged, its presence nevertheless assures the ultimate spiritual sovereignty and "eternity" of the Jewish people within creation.[12]

The "dominion" of the subject

The profound difference between the thought of Bacon and the Renaissance, on the one hand, and the Maharal, on the other, is in the relation to what has gone before. Bacon wrote the *Novum Organum* - the "*new* instrument" - which was built on the rejection of past thought. The pursuit of final causes and the syllogistic-deductive exposition of revealed or metaphysical truths was construed as the antithesis of his experimental and inductive method. Bacon sought (if not to deny, at least) to free the subject from any pre-conceived notions - that is, of any truth which preceded and was, in some sense, beyond or greater than the subject's mind. The concept of a transcendental objectivity is herewith put aside. The Maharal,

---

[11] *Likkutei Amarim* (transl. Nissan Mindel), second ed'n London: Kehos, 5740 (1980) ch, 37, p.173.

[12] Compare this to the notion, explained in later Chassidic thought, that soul enlivens the body, because it proceeds from G-dliness, which is "essentially living" (Rabbi Sholom Dov Ber of Lubavitch, *Sefer Ma'amarim* of the year 5666, N.Y: Kehos, p. 177).

on the other hand, in picturing the Jewish people as the transhistorical subject of history, is *not* displacing the notion of an objective reality represented by the transcendence of G-d or the notion of Divine Providence, which characterized the medieval Jewish philosophy of Maimonides. To the contrary, the Jewish people is to be comprehended as the first "ring" in the chain of creation itself. That is, the process of immanent vitalization of the creation by G-d, *passes through* the Jewish people. Through this enclothement of G-dliness *in* the Jewish people, they become the proximate source and vitality of the creation itself.

The significance of the Jewish people as the vehicle of G-dliness in creation is that through them *G-dliness* has been draws been *drawn down* into this world. To this corresponds a very important theological notion. This is the notion of immanent or indwelling G-dliness - termed in the language of the Kabalah and Chassidus, *memaleh*, the G-dliness which *fills* creation - as distinct from transcendent or encompassing *(sovev)* G-dliness which enlivens the Creation from without, *ex nihilo*. The indwelling G-dliness is in fact a ray, a modicum of infinite, transcendent G-dliness, which has entered the creation to become its internal vitality, its soul. Whilst creation represents the idea of contraction or concealment of G-dliness, nevertheless the G-dliness which enters within, to *become* concealed and received in a limited way, still has something of the quality and simplicity of transcendences.[13] The Jewish people are spiritually associated with transcendent G-dliness: like it, they are "removed" *(nivdal)* from the creation. At the

---

[13] See Rabbi M.M. Schneerson, *Sefer Ma'amarim Meluket*, Vol 3 (N.Y: Kehos, 1989 (5750)), pp. 232-233. Thus, immanent G-dliness has the qualities of transcendence and is itself unchanged by the "vessels" which receive it and structure a finite creation. The spiritual core of creation remains "simple" G-dliness, notwithstanding its being overlaid with numerous concealments, which have enabled its passage into immanence.

same time, however, they constitute the spiritual form, which finds its enclothement within the material *(chomer)* of creation. Thus it is that the Maharal represents the Jewish people as essentially *removed (nivdal)* from the creation receiving from *(mei'amitas)* G-dliness, whilst being in the creation, as its *tzura*, its soul, or spiritual form.

It is interesting that Chassidic teaching would call (in accordance with the Kabalah) this aspect of G-dliness enclothed in the creation, *malchus*[14], which may be translated as "kingship" or "dominion"; and Francis Bacon also treated the normative posture of the subject towards the object, nature (i.e. objective reality) as one of "dominion". Significantly, their positions are mutual opposites. For Bacon and the Renaissance, objectivity means nature in an utterly secular sense and it is to be conquered, *subdued* and made an appurtenance of the subject. Accordingly, any principles behind nature will simply be "natures" to be discovered by the subject. These principles have priority and importance only in the sense that nature must be "obeyed" *in order to* dominate it. Man's sovereignty is an end in itself, a *human* end, and the appropriation of nature is indeed the establishment of this sovereignty.[15]

In the perspective of the Maharal, on the other hand, the *dominion* of the Jewish people is the transference into the immanent plane of nature and history, of the supra-natural, transcendent Divine influence. The notion of Kingship in a practical legal sense in Torah bears out the function of

[14] See Tzemech Tzedek, *Sefer HaLikkutim*, N.Y.: Kehos, 1977, entry *"Shechina"* (sub-entry, *shechina ila'ah, shechina tata'ah*).

[15] Cf. Malherbe, *op. cit.*: "Therefore, if man is able to be the true interpreter of nature [and his understanding will truly adequate nature] . . . then he will be the master of nature, but so far as he is its minister." p. 97. It is this which will restore the dominion man possessed over nature before he "fell" (Cf. *Novum Organum* IV, 247-48, here cited by Malherbe).

"Kingship" or "Dominion" as a spiritual concept. A Jewish king, in the literal sense, simultaneously represents exaltedness *and* extreme self-nullification - majesty and receptivity. This is found in the seemingly opposite halachic requirements for a Jewish king that his honour and majesty is expressed in a multitude of ways and is unwaivable. He is the master of land and people. At the same time he must accompanied constantly, in all his comings and goings, by a scroll of the Law to remind him that he is solely the executive of the Divine Law and Will[16]. The Jewish people are the agency of G-*d's* dominion.

The difference between the Maharal - whose primary perspective is upon G-dliness *drawn into immanence* and the role of the Jewish people in the creation - and Maimonides - whose main perspective is that of *transcendental* G-dliness - is brought out by a critique of Maimonides made by the Maharal. We recall the discussion (in chapter 2) of the statement of Maimonides that G-d is the Knower, the Known and the Knowledge. For the Maharal[17], this statement is to be criticized on the grounds that one cannot ascribe any attribute to G-d, Whose being is beyond all description *whatsoever*. Knowledge or knowing is an attribute and a category which relates to creation. It is inapplicable to the Creator of all attributes and of all categories of creation.

Chassidic thought explains that the ostensible conflict between the Maharal and Maimonides is only one of *perspective* (and that their distinct perspectives are in fact complementary). Maimonides, taking up the perspective of transcendent G-dliness, looks at the way transcendent G-dliness "from above" *enclothes* itself in attributes. As in the case of a person putting on a garment, the garment does not

---

[16] See Maimonides, *Hilchos M'lochim*, chapters 1-3.

[17] See Second Introduction to *G'vuros HaShem*.

change the person *himself*. If it is a special uniform, the person seeks to achieve an *effect through* it. From the point of view of the *onlooker* (for which the analogy is that of the creation as *recipient* of Divine influence via the attributes) the person in new garb gives a wholly new impression, "comes over" differently. The onlooker knows that this is not the person himself, but a guise; and he cannot see the person itself beyond or within the guise. He can only assert that the guise is not the person. Thus, from the primary perspective of the Maharal, which is the perspective of the creation, *from below to above*, so to speak, it seems wholly inappropriate to project attributes innovated by G-d for the sake of the creation *onto* G-d. From this "earthly" perspective the G-dliness dressed in this instrumentation cannot be seen, and can only be grasped as being *not* this instrumentation - attributes. From the transcendent perspective of Maimonides, G-dliness *is* seen, but *dressed* in attributes, so that the attribute - and for Maimonides, the attributes such as "knowing", "willing", "living", "powerful" which are particularly *united* with G-d - can be grasped as being "associated" with G-d.

In the language of Chassidic thought, Maimonides assumes the perspective of the simple "light", an analogy for transcendent G-dliness, which enters the attributes *(s'firos)* and shines in an altered way through them. The Maharal, on the other hand, takes up the perspective of the attribute *(s'fira)* as a the "vessel" considered separate from the light, which hides or screens or refracts the light, unseen in its purity.[18] It is only

---

[18] See *Sefer Halikkutim* of the Chassidus of the *Tzemech Tzedek* (N.Y: Kehos, 1982), entry *"Hu hayodei'ah"* together with notes of the editor. Analogous to this is the question raised by the Tzemech Tzedek of how we can fulfill the injunction of the sages to pray "to Him and not to His attributes" when we find that the liturgy of *prayer itself* employs names of G-d referring to His attributes. The answer he gives is that we are in fact praying to G-d Himself as He appears "enclothed" in certain attributes. See *"Shoresh mitzvas tefillah"* in *Derech Mitzvosecho* (N.Y: Kehos).

the later development of Jewish thought which would elaborate and conceptually formulate the unity of both perspectives.[19]

2. The subject - and the function of morality

What strikes one strongly in certain facets of the "ethical philosophy" of the Renaissance is what looks, *in comparison* with the theological doctrines of the middle ages at least, like a strange *amoralism* or pragmatism. Nowhere is this more strongly brought out than in the writings of Niccolo Machiavelli (1469-1572). In raising up the spectre of the individual state against a universal natural order represented by the medieval government of the Catholic church, there is the rejection also of the ethos or philosophical doctrine of natural law which underlay that order. That, as seen in the previous chapter, was conceived as the result of a *"divinely* instilled" universal reason. Ethics, in the work of Machiavelli, align themselves with a new centre: man or the broader correlate of man, as against the universal order of the Church, namely the *individual sovereign state*. For just as, philosophically, the subject asserts itself, so too do individual states assert themselves against the medieval universal Church.

Burckhardt wrote of the individualism of Renaissance Italy that its self-centred morality is "in itself neither good nor bad, but necessary; within it has grown up a modern standard of good and evil - a sense of moral responsibility - which is essentially different from that which was familiar in the middle ages".[20] Machiavelli (anism) is a household name for amoral, manipulative conduct. Yet the fact that Machiavelli's work is

---

[19] See chapter 4.
[20] J. Burckhardt, *The Civilization of Renaissance in Italy* (in the Middlemore transl. of 1878), Oxford: Phaidon Press, 1944, p. 279.

part of the stock of civilization is an indication that it has some kind of moral core. Machiavelli was committed to the sovereignty of the state and his moral theory underlines this commitment. For Machiavelli's morality is to be comprehended and explained as functional to the *autonomy* of *man*. Machiavelli's prescription of conduct for the ruler is one designed to maintain the *health* of the *sovereign polity*. If measures will result in its disintegration they are to be shunned and therefore ". . . precepts of the moralists . . . are to be judged by their consequences"[21] for the well-being, the preservation of sovereignty. The notion of the maintenance of *human sovereignty*, as symbolized by the *maintenance* of the sovereign political state, is the objective against which morality must be functionally measured.

The key term of this morality is *virtu*. It has been translated in many ways - as "prowess", "valour", "audacity, "skill"", "civic spirit", "virtuosity", "ability". In Bernard Crick's words "a man is himself at his best [- embodying *virtu* -] when active for the common good".[22] As Crick writes: "*Virtu* is the quality of mind and action that creates, saves or maintains cities".[23] This is a constructive, formative ethic. "It is not virtu to destroy a city"[24]. "Vitality" and "energy"[25] are measures of human and state efficacy against corruption and tyranny.

Machiavelli's doctrine is not amoral inasmuch as it does not endorse abstract ethical precepts. Rather it is the ethic of vital

---

[21] Introduction by L. Walker to *The Discourses of Niccolo Machiavelli* (in Walker's translation) London: Routledge and Kegan Paul, 1950, Vol. I, p. 83. Quoted by B. Crick in introduction to, *Machiavelli: The Discourses* (ed. Bernard Crick, transl. L.J. Walker) Middlesex: Penguin, 1974

[22] *Machiavelli*: The Discourses (ed. Bernard Crick, transl. L.J. Walker) p.55.

[23] Introduction to Machiavelli: The Discourses, p. 58.

[24] Ibid.

and audacious human autonomy itself. Thus Machiavelli wrote:

> Our religion has glorified humble and contemplative men, rather than men of action. it has assigned as man's good humility, abnegation and contempt for worldly things, whereas the other identified with magnanimity, bodily strength and everything else that tends to make man very bold . . .[26]

Simply put, morality is that which invigorates and asserts sovereign subjectivity. It symbolizes vital human authorship.

Just as in Machiavelli morality relates to the vigour of the sovereign subject, so too, we find in the Maharal the notion that Torah - which sets out the ethical precepts, *mitzvos*, by which the Jewish people are to live - steers the special spiritual sovereignty of the Jewish people in the creation. The Torah sets forth practical precepts dealing with human thought, speech and deed; and yet the Torah relates *essentially* to a spiritual realm. This notion has also been expressed elsewhere in the terms that "the Torah speaks essentially in the supernal realms, and secondarily hints [its meanings] in the lower realms".[27] The inner senses of the mitzvos are spiritual concepts, which in their totality form a perfect unity, associated with the simplicity and oneness of G-dliness itself.

It is interesting to note that the Maharal[28] rejects Maimonides notion that the mitzvos are present in order to rectify attitudes

---

[25] See introduction of Hans Freyer to the German translation, *Der Fuerst* (transl. E. Merian-Genast), Stuttgart: Reclam, 1961 (rep. 1972), p. 18.

[26] *Discourses* II.2. Quoted by Crick, *op. cit.* p. 64.

[27] *Asora Ma'amoros, Ma'amar Chikur HaDin* 3:22, quoted in *Likkutei Sichos*, Vol. 23, p. 37.

[28] *Derech Chayim* on "*Rabbi Chananya*" at the end of first chapter of *Pirkei Avos*.

and to deal with the *yeitzer*, the perverse inclination, of man. Rather he presents the mitzvos as decrees of the King *(g'zeiros haMelech)*. That is to say, their reason is something which *cannot* be grasped, since the Torah originates from a spiritual sphere which *transcends* creation. Here, too, we can *reconcile* the views of the Maharal and of Maimonides by arguing similarly as above that Maimonides, for whom the supernal perspective or transcendent aspect of G-dliness is *obvious and manifest*, is able to contemplate the enclothement of the Divine enclothed in a world-rectifying and world-related function. For the Maharal, whose perspective is from "below", and for whom G-dliness has the characteristic that it is the unknown beyond, the *un*comprehended, it becomes important to assert the *transcendent* root of mitzvos. This parallels the difference between Maimonides and the Maharal in the matter of the Divine "attributes".

Having thus established that the Torah itself is something which is essentially removed from the creation, it will be understood that its function, so to speak, for the Jewish people is to achieve spiritual purity and to maintain their spiritual "form" *(tzura)*. Thus the purpose of the mitzvos *set out in* Torah, is purification of the soul and *attachment* to G-d, which attachment is also the reward of mitzvos.[29] The mitzvos of the Torah in their transcendent purity are the nexus of attachment of the Jewish people to G-d, through which they remain *nivdal*, removed from the creation. So it is that the *multiplicity* of (six hundred and thirteen) mitzvos given to the Jewish people relates to their attachment to transcendent G-dliness[30] whilst the seven mitzvos given to the nations represents their greater association with G-dliness immanent in nature. Moreover, just as spirituality - G-dliness - is one, so too the united totality of

---

[29] *Tiferes Yisroel*, ch. 9.
[30] *Tiferes Yisroel*, ch. 9.

the Jewish people is alone the worthy receptacle of Torah. For this reason the Torah was given only to the Jewish people when they were (actually) gathered in their *entirety* at Sinai and not earlier to the Patriarchs.[31]

In summary, the Renaissance morality of Machiavelli is functional to the sovereignty the human subject - symbolized by the sovereignty of the state. Morality promotes *virtu* - the vitality of the self-asserted subject. It rejects the "transcendent" objective order, represented by the government of the church. No objective spiritual realm (of which the universal medieval church had been the custodian) stands over the subject. Rather, objectivity has become secularized as *nature*; and subject has consciously made object its own; it has become the head of nature.

For the Maharal on the other hand, the Jewish people is found also in "nature" - on the plane of history and of interaction with the creation. Nevertheless its task is not to assure the vigour of man, the primacy of the subject over creation, as a goal in itself. Rather its purpose - though, and by virtue of, its cleaving to Torah and mitzvos - is to establish itself, as the form and reflector of transcendent G-dliness within the *creation* as a whole.

3. Redemption and the restoration of subjectivity

The concept of redemption in the Maharal again bears certain comparisons - and within those similarities, vital differences - with notions in Renaissance thought concerning the movement of history and the "justice" of history. Particularly instructive

---

[31] *Tiferes Yisroel*, ch. 17

in this regard is the concept of tragedy in Shakespeare's plays. Even though Shakespeare was not a philosopher, he is one of the greatest figures of Renaissance civilization; he embodied its values, and unquestionably a philosophy can be *extrapolated* from his plays, as has been done in the classic lecture of A.C. Bradley on "the substance of Shakespearean tragedy".[32] The Renaissance philosophy, found in Shakespeare, has to do with the secularization of objective reality as "nature" and the sense in which the subject, man, is inserted into it as its "head".

Bradley contrasts Shakespearean tragedy with a medieval notion of tragedy, "namely that man is blind and helpless, the plaything of an inscrutable power . . . which appears to smile on him for a little, and then on a sudden strikes him down in his pride".[33] Shakespearean tragedy, on the other hand, does not arise from an overwhelming sense of fate. Rather it proceeds in lines of causality from the deeds of man. Even though "chance" or "accident" play a role, they do not detract from, or at least nullify the consideration of the direction of their origin - human actions.[34] Moreover, action is a product of human *character*, of the good and bad in human character, which is an expression of inner struggle. The unbalanced and unreasoned act - "a marked one-sidedness . . . a fatal tendency to identify the whole being with one interest, object, passion, or habit of mind"[35] - is the source of tragedy, particularly when it is combined with a *nobility* of character. One senses the *waste* of good and this is what creates the sense of tragedy.

---

[32] In A.C. Bradley, *Shakespearean Tragedy*, London: Macmillan (Papermac ed'n), 1966 (first ed'n 1904).

[33] *Ibid.*, p. 4.

[34] *Ibid.*, p. 9.

[35] *Ibid.*, p. 13.

Consequences reach beyond the control of men. Actions lead to logically reconstructable but unforeseen circumstances and there is a certain opacity or obscurity, a "blank necessity" in the course of events initiated by man; but at the same time, Bradley points to the existence of a "moral order" or *power* in the universe of Shakespeare. This notion of the order of nature is not theological. Bradley describes the "attitude" of this order as one which

> . . . does not show itself indifferent to good and evil, or equally favourable or unfavourable to both, but shows itself akin to good and alien from evil . . . If it is chiefly evil that violently disturbs the order of the world, this order cannot be friendly to evil or indifferent between evil and good, any more than a body which is convulsed by poison is friendly to it or indifferent to the distinction between poison and good . . .[36]

Interestingly this picture of nature seems to be a mirror of the Renaissance vision of man in which good prevails basically over evil, and, notwithstanding its foibles, *wants* perfection. Moreover, evil wreaks havoc like poison does to the body which ultimately - if even by means of convulsion - *expels* it. Indeed, evil can only be sustained by the goodness which cohabits with it, so that when evil masters a person its also destroys him. This nature is not only a mirror of man; it seems also to be an extension or an external correlate of him. Nature is the larger body *of* man: and it exists in a *systemic relationship* with man. His evil produces the convulsions in nature, which affect him: ". . . the persons whom this evil inhabits, are not really something outside this order... they are within it and a part of it."[37] The behaviour of nature reveals it as a continuum with man:

---

[36] Ibid., p. 25.
[37] Ibid. , p. 27.

We remain confronted with the inexplicable fact, or the no less inexplicable appearance, of a world travailing for perfection, but bringing to birth, together with glorious good, an evil which it is able to overcome only by self-torture and self-waste. And this fact or appearance is tragedy.[38]

In the Maharal we find also a *systemic* sense of the relationship of the Jewish people with creation, in which they represent a sovereign spiritual form. The constructs and models of the Maharal suggest logical relationships - *causality, order, process* - between the spiritual and the material conditions of creation. This is not in the Shakespearean, humanist sense of man in nature, but in the sense of a *logic of G-dliness* within creation, which takes in the special character and place of the Jewish people. Thus, one of the most basic notions in the Maharal appears to be the concept of the *abnormality* of exile. it contradicts the "natural" spiritual sovereignty of the Jewish people within the creation. They should not be dispersed and subject to other nations, for even in the aberrant state of exile, they are inwardly and essentially one, and the spiritual centre of creation. It is sin which caused this dispersion and disintegration; but sin itself is "accidental"[39] to the essential goodness and sanctity residing within the Jewish people which will be, and historically has been, *manifested* when they are gathered together in their land with the Holy Temple standing. Exile is none other than the disintegration, the dispersion of the collective body *(k'lal)* of the Jewish people. The spiritual form of the Jewish people is one, just as G-d, Whose sanctity is associated with Israel, is one; and when that oneness of the Jewish people is not manifest, there is also, as Chassidic

---

[38] *Ibid.*, p. 29.

[39] "Exile is on account of sin and sin is also accidental" *Netzach Yisroel*, ch. 31.

philosophy would explain it, the exile of the *Shechina*[40], the unredeemed state of the creation as a whole.

Just as exile and the outward disintegration of the spiritual form of the Jewish people signify one another, so too the realization of that spiritual form requires them to be removed from the nations. When they are separated from the nations they are like fire which can dry out water - that is to say all that is undesirable amongst the nations. And when they are not separated but mixed, then the fire is extinguished by the water. The nature of freedom is not to be bound to another and the freedom and sovereignty of the Jewish people requires that it must be "in its place, for there is no connection of mergence between it and the nations."[41]

Divinely guided history is ultimately restorative of this order and it is *impossible* that exile should continue indefinitely. The human agent of redemption is Moshiach (the Messiah), who practically achieves the redemption of the world as a whole. But there is a Divine power or a spiritual logic in creation, which works to achieve the Messianic moment. For G-d, from Whom comes the existence of the world and its sustained being, it is improper that there should be destruction and loss, namely the destruction of the Temple, except that this should lead to a loftier state . . .[42]

So there functions, according to the Maharal, a *ko'ach ham'kabeitz*[43], a gathering or reconstitutive power within the

---

[40] Where it has been "lowered" so to speak, so as to impart its vitality to elements of impurity and strife.

[41] Ibid., ch. 24

[42] Ibid, ch. 26.

[43] Ibid., ch. 1.

Jewish people, which works against the unnatural, "unwell" state of exile. History is not then in Shakespearean Renaissance terms the straightening out of *human* justice through the catharsis of "man's" body, nature. It does not weather and painfully resolve the flaws of *human* character. Rather the logic of events has to do - through the travails of exile - with the restoration of the spiritual centre of the creation, the unity of the Jewish people, and the manifestation of their spiritual form, which is associated with the redemption of the world as a whole.

CHAPTER 4

THE ABSOLUTE
RABBI SCHNEUR ZALMAN OF LIADI
AND G.W.F. HEGEL

The historical novelty of Hegel's thought for Adorno is that it sought to mediate *the assertive subjectivity of Renaissance and Enlightenment thought with a distinct sense of the life of the object, "being", "substance" or "nature". In Hegel, subjectivity and objectivity become facets of an overarching or larger whole, "subject-object" or the Absolute. Rabbi Schneur Zalman of Liadi sets forth an analogous idea in the realm of Jewish thought. Immanent, "contracted" G-dliness, expressing an intelligible logic, and transcendent G-dliness are understood as being comprised or encompassed within an altogether higher level - absolute or quintessential - G-dliness (Atzmus). They find "identity" with one another, inasmuch as they are powers coordinated by* Atzmus *in the act or process of creation.*

The Absolute in Hegel works through a dialectical progression. Its goal is its self-manifestation as the "transparent" totality and system of all its moments, where the object is seen to have come into totally and concretely articulated identity with the subject. Here the infinite and the universal (the quality of the object) is experienced in the finite and the particular (the determinations achieved by the subject). In Rabbi Schneur Zalman's thought, Atzmus reveals Itself through the irradiation of transcendent G-dliness (in its full transcendence) within (immanently) every, even the "lowest", facet of finite creation.

This goal of the Hegelian Absolute is bound up with the dialectic of "externalization" and the return (or "taking up") of "externalization". In the thought of Rabbi Schneur Zalman, the process which leads to the manifestation of Atzmus, in the redemption, is the Jewish people's historical service of refinement of the creation. This is achieved through a "dialectic" of coercion (iscafia) of the finite and material, followed by its transfomation (is'chapcha), so as to express within it the transcendent.

1. The Absolute and the unity of subject and object

Hegel: the Absolute as subject-object

The years 1790 - or if we will take this back one year to the French Revolution in 1789 - to 1830, represents an epoch which held out, in the view of Adorno[1], the possibility of the fulfilment of the true promise of the Enlightenment. This was so politically, economically and philosophically. These years represent the greater part of the lifetime and productivity of Georg Wilhelm Friedrich Hegel, the work of whom states decisive features of *modern* philosophy. They are also years during which one of the great figures of Chassidic thought, Rabbi Schneur Zalman of Liadi (1745-1812), the first of the "Lubavitcher" Rebbeim (or Grand Rabbis), wrote and flourished.

The *political* epoch associated with these years is that of "enlightened Absolutism" injected with new conceptions of freedom and human autonomy. Both Hegel and Rabbi Schneur Zalman related to Napoleon, the great implementer of the secular ideals of the Enlightenment. Hegel called him the "*Weltgeist* on horseback". Rabbi Schneur Zalman, fleeing from the approach of Napoleon, sent back a messenger to fetch his slippers, which he had left behind, so that not even these should come into the possession of Napoleon.[2]

Economically and technically, the epoch was also a portentous one: it was the time of the industrial revolution[3], which opened up the *concrete* possibility of man's actual

---

[1] Theodor W. Adorno, "Theorie der Halbbildung", Gesammelte Schriften, Bd. 8 (Frankfurt am Main: Suhrkamp, 1972), p.106

[2] The messenger was also instructed to burn the house to the ground.

[3] See T.S. Ashton, The Industrial Revolution 1760-1830 (London: Oxford University Press, first edition 1948), who focuses on the industrial revolution in England.

sovereignty over nature. The winning of the control of nature itself, the disclosure and making over of *all its powers* to man, found its place in the context of a new theory of political economy. That which for the Renaissance was a *project* is undertaken by Enlightenment thought as its work in progress. Just as Napoleonic doctrine is for Hegel a model of the political concept of freedom, so is Adam Smith's *Wealth of Nations*, which was published first in 1776, the foundation of Hegel's concept of political economy and is the context in which human freedom must be understood.

Hegel's *Philosophy of Right* relates the fulfillment of human freedom to the developed form of modern "civil society" based on modern political economy. This is an organization of man's productive engagement with nature - via a division of labour and based on principles of contract - geared to the satisfaction of human needs. This engagement with nature, however, is an arrangement in which man is not simply inserted into the economic instruments of the satisfaction of needs, but is rather their master. Civil society, allows man to "return" to himself, and to be truly free, because it is reduced to the status of an instrument for the fulfillment of his needs and the mutual regulation of welfare. Man has engaged with, and organized nature with the advent of modern civil society, but is not lost in that engagement: he is sovereign over it.[4]

Hegel's philosophy in general represents a triumphalism of the subject not found in the Renaissance or earlier Enlightenment thought. The Renaissance asserted the primary value of man and human knowledge. Man - not theology - was the navigator of the universe. But he was a navigator over a

---

[4] See Joachim Ritter, *Hegel and the French Revolution - Essays on the Philosophy of Right*, translated by Richard Dien Winfield, Cambridge, Mass.: MIT Press, 1982, pp. 76ff.

void. The void - nature[5] - was to be embarked upon boldly, valiantly, not without risk of tragedy. The subject *imposed* itself upon object, nature, treating it as its extension or appurtenance - its own body. The Enlightenment - in such great and diverse figures as David Hume and Immanuel Kant - *steps back* to reflect upon the forms and limits of the subject's knowledge. Kant's work first contains a reflection upon the *categories* of understanding. A further feature of the Kantian philosophy, pertinent to this point, is the concept of the "thing in itself" over against the categories of the subject's understanding. This produces the somewhat paradoxical gulf between *phenomena*, construed knowledge or understanding and *numena*, the things in themselves. How the two realms are to be reconciled is an issue for the Kantian philosophy - how can we know whether knowledge is *true*: whether subject adequates object? At all events, the extensive reflection upon the constitution of the subject's apparatus of understanding is a confirmation of - a statement of confidence in - the efficacy of the subject in its dealings with reality.

In Hegel, the subject gains dramatically in relation to the object, which Kant somewhat agnostically conceived as the "thing in itself". With Hegel, Renaissance and Enlightenment dualism or scepticism - both relating to the *solitariness* of the subject "within" or "before" the object - is replaced by the full-scale appropriation by the subject of, or rather its *merger* with, the object. It is the completion of the Copernican transformation of medieval philosophy, for which metaphysical, a divinely administered order of *being*, has been reduced simply to an object *for* the subject. Hegel follows on

---

[5] The Renaissance's secularized version of the Divine basis of "being", as discussed earlier.

from Kant, but also goes significantly beyond Kant[6]. With Hegel, the subject has dressed itself in reality and reality concretely expresses the subject.

The figure of Hegelian thought which establishes the groundwork for Marx and *modern* social theory - the philosophy of praxis or action - is a notion of the "Whole" or "Absolute", as the *identity* of subject and object: *subject-object*. Both Hegel and Marx, take up the perspective of an Absolute or total historical process, which incorporates subject and object, man and nature, in the one identical whole. In Hegel this is the figure of "mental substance" *(geistige Substanz)*, set forth in the Forward of the *Phenomenology of Mind*; in Marx it is the nexus of man and nature presented in Marx's mature economic and political writings as the historical "form of production". That is to say, we come to the concept of an overarching "process" containing a "mediation" of subjectivity with objectivity, thought and being as two sides of the one - dialectical - process. Through this man truly appropriates nature: he comes to himself as the true master, the human visage of nature.

Adorno saw both the promise and failure to actuate the promise of the Enlightenment in Hegel's philosophy, precisely in this issue. For the mediation of subjectivity and objectivity involved, in Adorno's words, the task of joining the necessarily *identifying* reason of the subject with the *non-identical* (different and non-definable) quality of the object. In Hegel one finds the adoption of the *mysterium magnum* - in Aquinas' terms the "infinite ocean of substance": but not in the sense that the subject itself defers *to*, and demurs before, this metaphysical objectivity; for in Hegel the object is

---

[6] Some wish to argue that a comparable development is projected also in the late and posthumously published philosophy of Kant. See. F. Copleston, *A History of Philosophy*, Vol. 6 Part II, ch. 16.

appropriated and inhabited by the subject. Hegel, in positing the concept of the identity of subject and object, makes every determination by the subject a determination of the objective reality. This completes the secularization of being: the signal quality *of the* object - its "infinitude" - has been rendered *finite*. The object is made in the image of the subject. Georg Lukacs put it thus:

Hegel's philosophy, notwithstanding all his protests, is overwhelmingly pantheistic . . . The advantage of pantheism was that it gave German idealists the opportunity to analyze objective reality, both nature and society, in a scientific manner, i.e. according to their own immanent laws; it enabled them to reject out of hand all appeals to another world, while permitting them to construct a general system in which their idealist principles could achieve their necessary philosophical consummation in G-d . . . We are reminded of Schopenhauer's *mot* that pantheism is the polite form of atheism, a polite strategem for bowing G-d out of the universe.[7]

This, however, goes further than pantheism: it has made *man* G-d. Napoleon in Hegel's words was *Weltgeist* ("world-spirit"), a fusion of man and the material world. He was the personal incorporation of the Absolute: or the practical Hegel, whose philosophical consciousness is that of the Absolute. In the words of Alexandre Kojeve,

The phenomenon that completes the historical evolution and thus makes the absolute Science possible, therefore, is the "conception" *(Begreifen)* of Napoleon by Hegel. This dyad, formed by Napoleon and Hegel, is the perfect Man, fully and definitively "satisfied" by what he is and by what he *knows*

---

[7] Georg Lukacs, *The Young Hegel. Studies in the Relations between Dialectics and Economics* (transl. R. Livingstone), London: Merlin Press, 1975.

himself to be. *This* is the realization of the ideal revealed by the myth of Jesus . . ., of the G-d-Man. And that is why Hegel completes Chapter VI with these words: "*Es ist* der erscheinende G-tt . . ."; "*This* is the revealed G-d" . . .[8]

Rabbi Schneur Zalman: quintessential G-dliness and the act of creation

In a fundamental work of Rabbi Schneur Zalman of Liadi, the *Sha'ar Hayichud v'ho'emunah*[9], we find a comparable notion of the joining of the dimensions of subjectivity and objectivity and their inclusion in a higher level. This is the notion of immanent and transcendent G-dliness as "powers" of a level in G-dliness called *Atzmus*, literally "Itselfness" - absolute or quintessential G-dliness. As briefly adumbrated above, this is a level which is beyond both any positive (immanent) or negative (transcendent) apprehension. It is the source of both. Nevertheless this is also termed a level in G-d*liness*: we can somehow relate to this as "negation of the positive and negation of the negative", but as for G-d Himself, "we cannot even open our mouths", as the saying goes amongst Chassidim.

It is alone within the province of *Atzmus* to create *ex nihilo*, something from nothing. The act of creation employs both the above mentioned powers. These are powers not in the sense that they inhere in *Atzmus*, but have been fashioned by *Atzmus* as instruments of the act of creation. One is the transcendent power, engendering all being into existence from nothing. This power is continuously applied: creation is not something which

---

[8] Alexandre Kojeve, *Introduction to the Reading of Hegel (Lectures on the* Phenomenology of Spirit, assembled by Raymond Quenau, edited by Allan Bloom, translated from the French by J.H. Nichols, Jr.), N.Y: Basic Books, 1969 p. 70.

[9] Generally included in the work *Tanya* as its second part.

happened once, and from that point continues to live its own existence independent of its Creator. In this respect, it is not like the artisan's artifact, which continues to exist independently, when the artisan leaves his workplace and goes out into the street. Rather, creation in all the multitude of its entities is something which needs to be re-engendered - reanimated - in every moment, such that with the withdrawal of the creative force it would instantly revert to absolute nothingness[10]. This transcendent creative power, which might be called *objective* - in the sense that it establishes the *objective being* of creation - is equal in all things: it founds the common fact of their existence and is formally "indifferent" to the differences between the multiplicity of phenomena, entities, making up creation.

Were this transcendent, *infinite* generative power to be the sole power in the act of creation, it would result in comparably infinite creations. Here Rabbi Schneur Zalman also invokes a concept from the Kabalah, that of *Tzimtzum*, or "contraction", to account for the existence of the *finite* and differentiated entities of creation. The G-dly power of contraction comes into play - to invoke metaphors of Chassidic and Kabalistic thought - in order to screen out, or filter, the "light" (again a metaphor) of transcendent or infinite, engendering G-dliness, such as to "hew out" or to "inscribe" within it, finite creations[12]. It is the principle of "contraction" or delimitation which produces a *finite* creation to exist, with a contracted "quantity" of G-dliness becoming its immanent

---

[10] *Sha'ar HaYichud v'ho'emunah*, ch. 1.

[11] Rabbi Schneur Zalman does not refer to it in this way, but we term it such in the sense in which it may be compared to notions of secular thought.

[12] See the notes by Rabbi Menachem Mendel Schneerson on chapter 10 of the *Sha'ar HaYichud v'ho'emunah* in J. Korf, *Likkutei Bi'urim besefer haTanya*, N.Y.,1974.

vitality, the "soul" *("nefesh")* of the particular entity. Theletters, constituting the names in the "Holy Tongue", Hebrew, of things, themselves represent the principle of *tzimtzum*. The *name* of an entity in the Holy Tongue encodes the specific *tzimtzum* or contraction required to produce that entity. In the terms we have used thus far, this power could be called *subjective* insofar as it *systematically articulates in the objective* metaphysical foundation - the transcendent enlivening force - of being, the forms of the things of creation.

In the notion of the coordination of these powers by *Atzmus*, there is a further vital point in the doctrine of Rabbi Schneur Zalman. This is that the contraction or limitation by virtue of which the transcendent becomes immanent is not a *real* contraction or a limitation of the infinite engendering force[13]. It is not that the created entity is finite and it is simply enlivened from *without*, remaining separate from that infinite engendering force which brings it into, and holds it in, being. Rather, within the finite - or *together with* it - the infinite operates. As stated above, finite form is inscribed within the infinite force without the infinitude of the engendering power being in any way *actually* contracted. The phenomenon of contraction and concealment of the infinite thus appears as a reality only to the creation itself, and indeed, the concealment is effected so that the created entity should not be nullified in its existence by "exposure" to the infinite power. In reality, the finite and infinite coexist in the "Divine speech" or *fiat* bringing the individual entities of creation into, and holding them in, existence.

With this we can come to understand the Chassidic conception of the Absolute in relation to the "identity" of subjectivity and objectivity, of the finite (the categorical) and the infinite: both

---

[13] As elucidated in *Likkutei Sichos*, Vol. 25, pp. 200ff.

meet in the process of creation itself, which, however, is the province of *Atzmus*, their source. Neither the *primary* perspectives of Maimonides nor of the Maharal of Prague - which are those of transcendent and immanent G-dliness respectively - contradict this higher, *third* perspective of *Atzmus*. We could perhaps say that Rabbi Schneur Zalman takes up the "subjective" immanent perspective of the Maharal - of the creation itself as reflecting the worldly, delineable and cognizable, logic of G-dliness - and the elusive *objective* transce quintessential G-dly act of creation. aimonides and shows how these are joined in the ongoing *quintessential* G-dly act of creation.

In Rabbi Schneur Zalman's conception, there is, therefore, no simple *identity* between the power of "contraction" associated with *immanent* nature or creation and the *transcendent* engendering power, as we find in the Hegelian subject-object. And certainly the Absolute *is not* the "fusion" of these two dimensions, as is the Hegelian Absolute. It is true that something like "identity" is intimated in the statement that the "transcendent G-d *is* the immanent G-d" - *Havayeh hu ho'Elokim*[14] - found in the prayer *Oleinu* and which is the culminating acknowledgment of the service of Yom Kippur. But by this is not meant a conflation of the transcendent and the immanent. Rather, its meaning is that quintessential G-dliness *(Atzmus)*, which acts through a transcendent power is the *same* quintessential G-dliness which acts through the power of contraction and limitation.

The act of creation *ex nihilo*, which has no likeness whatsoever in the creation itself, is thus a *process* which coordinates the powers of infinite, transcendent engendering and of finite,

---

[14] *Havayeh* is a reordering of the letters of the tetragrammaton, connoting the transcendent power, and *Elokim* the name designating the power of contraction.

delimiting, form-giving. Moreover - and here is the main point - because *Atzmus* is that which creates, so also the created entity itself is something which is quintessential in that its true being is the quintessential G-dly act *enclothed* within the entity. The existence of the individual entity is the Divine speech, the act of Divine creation[15]. Since the Creator of the item is ultimately - not transcendent or immanent but rather - quintessential G-dliness, consequently, in the words of Chassidus, the created existence *is* the quintessential existence (of G-dliness). Hegel, however, turned this proposition around and changed the positions of subject and predicate. For Hegel the concrete creation - world-history, world-historical figures, world consciousness - is the revelation of the Absolute. In the doctrine of Rabbi Schneur Zalman, the creation *reflects* G-dliness in its highest manifestation, *Atzmus*, inasmuch as it discloses the *quintessential act of creation itself*. For Hegel, G-d is concrete; for Rabbi Schneur Zalman, the concrete is G-dly.

2. The manifested Absolute

Hegel: the unity of universal and the particular

The character of the Hegelian dialectic is essentially that it is the mediation of subjectivity and objectivity *within* the complex of the subject-object, "spiritual substance" or the Whole *(das Ganze)*. Objectivity is now one side of the total subject-object, just as is subjectivity. The dialectical movement within the whole is that whole "moves" from a state of relative abstraction and generality (its objective aspect, whether as

---

[15] *Ibid*. p. 202. Many stories illustrate this notion. When Rabbi Schneur Zalman lay on his death bed, he pointed to a rafter in the ceiling and asked his grandson, who was to be known as the *Tzemach Tzedek*, what he saw. When his grandson said that he saw a rafter, Rabbi Schneur Zalman stated that all he could see was the "Divine word" animating, and in the truest sense, *constituting* the rafter.

"being" or some further articulated level of generality and universality) into a new concretization or particularization. This is achieved by the subject side of the Whole, that which posits, determines, according to the categories of the idea, or mind. The next stage of the dialectic is to return this level of particularity, experienced as self-externalization, as being "other", to be united within the whole. The Whole - subject-object - in this stage returns to be "with" or "by" itself. Thus, in the broadest schema of the Hegelian *Enclyclopaedia of the Philosophical Sciences*, the *Logic*, the "idea" - for Hegel, "the thought of G-d before the creation" - subsequently expresses and *externalizes* itself as nature, the "Philosophy of Nature" being the second part of his system. This is a movement into definition, particularization, materialization. The third stage in this macrocosm of the dialectic is to "return" the particularized externalization, nature, and to fuse it with its original general concept, the idea. The third part of the Hegelian system is thus the philosophy of Mind, which presents the fully articulated identity of thought and being - of subject and object as the existence of man in *society* and as the (philosophical encyclopaedic) sequence of sciences which reflect the planes of his moral and social existence. These take in man as a psychological, anthropological, social, economic, legal, and at a higher level - in the "sciences of the Absolute" - his artistic, religious and ultimately philosophical being.

In general the dialectic, not only at this broadest level, but through each level and sub-level (and so on) goes through a process of movement from generality or universality to particularization to the unification of the general and the particular. Thus the whole is constantly articulating itself, and then returning its articulated or externalized form, such that this particular articulation should be comprehended as a *moment* - or phase - *of the whole*. In other words, the significance of the "march" of the dialectic is that as it proceeds through its general stages (the idea, nature, "mind" as a social entity) and the sub-stages within these general stages, it has defined the *whole* of reality, and comprehended the multitude of its specific contents as *in relation to the* whole. It is "concept" as the articulated "allness" of truth. Particularity in its *fullness* has been brought back into identity with universality. This is the standpoint of the Absolute Idea, incorporated in the philosophical self-consciousness of the Hegelian system. In this reflection upon, or remembrance *(Erinnerung)* of, all the completed stages of dialectic, the articulated moments, the transparency of the whole is achieved. When there is no lacuna which has not been *determined and then comprehended* as a moment of the whole, the Absolute - subject-object - comes to itself: it is *manifested*. Hegel in places ascribes to the Whole or universality the quality of "infiniteness". With the accomplished destination of the dialectic, the infinite is seen to inhabit every detail.

In the work of the mature Karl Marx[16], whose writings import strong Hegelian elements, we have the derivative expression of the Hegelian notion of externalization and its return or overcoming. Each historical engagement of man with nature has entailed class relationships which have alienated humans from a universality of community and freedom. Communism - the realization of universal community and freedom, in and through mankind's engagement with nature in production - comes about only as the *result* of a long historical *process*. The significance of the sequence of the stages of production - primitive communism, slavery, feudalism and capitalism - is that they represent the progressive appropriation of nature, objective human involvements with, and self-externalizations in, nature. Capitalism represents a cumulative

---

[16] As distinct from his early writings, to which we shall refer in the next chapter.

historical development in the mastery of nature - a colonization of the whole world - and the potential to supply all human needs and fully to make over nature's powers to man. At the same time, according to Marx, it concentrates the ownership of all these powers into an ever smaller group or ruling class, forming at the same time a universal, disenfranchised class: the proletariat. Consequently, the communist revolution, which occurs at the height of the development of capitalism, hands over the consolidated and integrated mastery of nature, achieved by the entire history of technical, economic and political history to a class equalized in the powerlessness of its members. With the revolution, universal alienation becomes universal individual freedom and sovereignty. But without capitalism and all previous stages of social and economic development, communism would not be possible. It *redeems*, and makes sense of, the long history of alienation through the progressive stages of man's appropriation of nature.

Rabbi Schneur Zalman: a "dwelling [for quintessential G-dliness] in the lower realms".
We have already introduced the notion, elaborated in the writings of Rabbi Schneur Zalman, of *Tzimtzum*, or "contraction", of G-dliness. This is a condition of a finite creation itself, and it explains, from the perspective of the creation, the *appearance* of a separation between creation and the G-dliness which engenders it. There has to be contraction of G-dliness in order that a created world should come into being - and further, progressive *Tzimtzumim* in order to articulate all the descending hierarchies of phenomena in creation - so that the creaturely should not be nullified in its existence by exposure to the infinite, engendering G-dly power. But, by the same token, the purpose of man in creation, having been situated in a creation made possible by *Tzimtzum*, is

ultimately to *transform* the *Tzimtzum*: that is, whilst maintaining the identity of finite things created through *tzimtzum*, so to refine and remake the material creation as to admit the infinite into the finite.

The notion of the fusion of infinite and finite found an *example* in a miracle found in the Holy Temple[17]. It is known that the inner sanctum of the Temple, called the "Holy of Holies" contained within it the Holy Ark, which in the first Temple contained the Tablets of the Law received by Moses on Sinai. This chamber, in the centre of which was placed the Ark of the law, measured twenty cubits by twenty cubits. It was found that when one measured from one side of the Holy Ark to the adjacent wall, the distance was 10 cubits. So, too, from the each of the sides of the Ark to its neighbouring wall of the Holy of Holies there were 10 cubits. It turned out that the Ark, which separately measured two-and-a-half cubits in length, took up no space at all. It possessed measure - as a *natural* phenomenon - and *no* measure at the same time. It was the transcendence of nature *within* nature. The holy Temple was a sufficiently refined "vessel" that this manifestation of *Atzmus* should occur within it.

The ultimate goal of creation, however, is elaborated in by Rabbi Schneur Zalman in terms of the words of our Sages that the "Holy One blessed be He desired a dwelling place for Himself in the lower realms". The redemptive goal of creation envisages the manifestation of *Atzmus* not simply in the holiest place in creation - in the unique sanctuary of the Holy Temple - but in the *lower* realms. This is explained by Rabbi Schneur Zalman and subsequent Chassidic writing to refer even to a realm, lower than which no other exists, in the sense of its

---

[17] See Talmud, tractate *Yoma* 21a.

[18] Tanya *(Likkutei Amarim)*, ch. 36.

obscuration and contraction of - and even its "antagonism" to - G-dliness. The "proof" of the oneness of G-dliness in the creation must be specifically where that which would otherwise appear to be in complete contradiction to it, acknowledges and, moreover, becomes a vessel or vehicle for it. For the manifestation of quintessential G-dliness as that which engenders and enlivens *all*, is that it must be *seen* to be the foundation of *everything*, just as the Absolute in the philosophy of Hegel, cannot be contradicted by anything, since everything is part of, and participates in, it.

The notion that *Atzmus* is truly manifest only when it is manifest in everything - the concept of a dwelling place for G-d in the lower realms - is understood by reference to the ordinary, mundane sense of a "dwelling". This is the sense that a dwelling is only then a dwelling - a dwelling of the one to whom it belongs - when ite that a dwelling is only then a dwelling - a dwelling of the one to whom it belongs - when it is wholly within his domain, when he feels "free" in all of it. When, that is to say, *every* part of it is his and he feels free to manifest himself in every part. So it is here, as adumbrated above, that the notion of a dwelling place for G-dliness comes about only when every concealment over every facet of creation has been transformed. Quintessential G-dliness is *wholly* disclosed, manifest. The Hebrew term for the exodus from Egypt *(yetzias Mitzrayim)* is thus explained to be cognate with the *yetzias Meiwer* realms"are spiritual ones. So long as infinite G-dliness, is yet obscured by any specific *tzimtzum* or limit and does not yet irradiate the creation in that facet, the dwelling place for G-dliness has not been achieved.

The great difference between the secular and Chassidic notions of the manifested Absolute is to be found the name to be given to this Absolute. For Hegel and Marx, it is man, who has wholly and freely appropriated nature; for Rabbi Schneur Zalman, it is quintessential G-dliness, Which has manifested

Itself, in the marriage of the finite and infinite in the "dwelling place" for G-dliness "in the lower realms".

3. The realization of the Absolute

Hegel: externalization and its overcoming
Crucial to the Hegelian philosophy is the sense of the dialectic as *process*. Dialectic, which runs through the general phases of the subject-object (being *in itself* as generality, self-externalization as mediated particularity – being *for itself* - and being *in and for itself* in the *return* of externalization and the unification of the general and the particular) is a continuing process. It means that subject-object, eventually understood as Mind, must travel through all the spheres of reality until it has finally externalized itself and defined itself each of these, and has *taken back* each of these externalizations as moments *of the whole*. Thus it takes on the form of an *Encyclopaedia* - a dialectically ordered sequence - *of the philosophical[ly comprehended] sciences*. In the previous section, we considered the notion of the manifested Absolute as the unity of subject and object: how it is that subject has marshalled all the object within itself - how substance has been fully inhabited by subject. That is the concept of *completed* process: here, however, our focus is on the dialectical progress, by which subject comes to *acquire* object, to *become* actually unified with it.

In this the key notion is that of "externalization" (*Entaeusserung*) and the return of the externalization. The idea here is that the subject passes from a stage of generality and universality to externalize itself in reality, as a form of reality which it fashions and comprehends. But this is its being reflected in a kind of "otherness". The movement into objectivity is mediated by specific forms: it lacks the freedom and universality of the general. It is engaged, but it is not fully "itself" in this engagement, and this is its unfreedom. True freedom, on the other hand is the integration of this outer existence back into oneself: it means to be involved with objectivity but also to be a *master* of one's involvement with the object.

The dialectical process in Hegel is set forth in the *Phenomenology of Mind* in the striking figure of a struggle between "Master and Slave", with the ultimate historical desideratum of the person (the "citizen") who embodies the *unity of master and slave*. The "slave" is occupied with formative work with objective reality. He has been inserted into, given over to it. It is not his, that he should be able reflectively to enjoy it, but rather it belongs to the master. But at the same time it is the special quality and *satisfaction* of the slave, that truth and value are attained through his work. The Master, on the other hand, can never be *satisfied* by what he *is*. Alexandre Kojeve summarizes this as follows:

> The Master can either make himself *brutish* in pleasure or *die* on the field of battle as Master, but he cannot *live consciously* with the knowledge that he is *satisfied* by what he is. Now, it is only conscious satisfaction, *Befriedigung*, that can complete History, for only the Man who *knows* he is *satisfied* by what he is no longer strives to go beyond himself, to go beyond what he is and what is, through Action that transforms Nature, through Action that creates History. If History must be *completed*, if absolute Knowledge must be possible, it is only the Slave who can do it, by attaining Satisfaction. And that is why Hegel says that the "truth" (= revealed reality) of the Master is the Slave. The human ideal, born in the Master, can be *realized* and revealed, can become *Wahrheit* (truth) only in and by Slavery.

To be able to stop and understand himself, a man must be *satisfied*. And for this, of course, he must cease to be a *Slave*. But to be able to cease being *Slave*, he must have *been* a Slave.

And since there are Slaves only where there is a Master, Mastery, while itself an *impasse*, is "justified" as a necessary stage of the historical existence that leads to the absolute Science of Hegel. The Master appears only for the sake of engendering the Slave who "overcomes" *(aufhebt)* him as Master, while thereby "overcoming" himself as Slave. And this Slave who has been "overcome" is the one who will be satisfied by what he is and will understand that he is satisfied in and by Hegel's philosophy, in and by the *Phenomenology*. The Master is only the "catalyst" of the History that will be realized, completed, and "revealed" by the Slave or the ex-Slave who has become a Citizen.[19]

"Master" symbolizes generality and universality; "slave" the aspect of self-externalization and particularity. In terms of Hegel's *Philosophy of Right*, these relate to abstract human rights and freedom, and the division of labour which is required concretely to achieve them. But the goal of autonomous civil society, sketched in the last section, is only the result of a social-historical travail and process: something which not the earlier Enlightenment, but only the era ushered in by Napoleon, was claimed to have achieved.

In Marx's historical or dialectical materialism, we find also a dialectic of externalization and its "return". The Hegelian subject-object becomes in the work of Marx the engagement of man with nature known as the process of production. The productive process, in the moment of its externalization, becomes for Marx the condition of *alienation* of a producing class from the conscious, political control of its *work*. Marx brings the Hegelian dialectic into a *material perspective* in that the redemption of man-productively-engaged-with-nature comes not through the abolition of that engagement, but

---

[19] *Op. cit.*, p. 47.

through the taking back of its *external* character: that is to say, by making over or transforming the nature of that engagement. Indeed these Marxian concepts are anticipated by Hegel in the *Philosophy of Right*, as Joachim Ritter characterizes its notion:

> As a world of labour mediated through objects of the will, modern society frees man not only from the power of nature, but simultaneously elevates freedom to the universal principle though the determination of labour and of all labour relations in such a form that skills can be alienated as objects of the will and property for a limited time; it releases to the person in himself, as personality, his selfhood and its realization. Therefore employer and labourer also no longer act towards one another as master and slave in the state of nature, but as persons.[20]

Thus, realized freedom consists in the notion that man has fulfilled his needs through the organization of nature in a system of political economy of which civil society is the complete expression. But in his engagement with nature, he is not "lost" in this externalization of himself. Rather, he has returned to himself, wholly conscious of himself as master of this relationship.[21] The *paticularity* of man's situation - as inserted in the economic subjugation of nature and the obtaining of his needs - now corresponds to the state of his full *universal* freedom.

---

[20] Ritter, *op. cit.*, p. 141.

[21] Compare here Marx's statement in the *Grundrisse* that man in the emancipated society is simply "restricted to watching and supervising the production process . . ." Karl Marx, *Selected Writings* (ed. D. McLellan) Oxford: O.U.P., 1977, p. 380.

Rabbi Schneur Zalman: the transformation of creation (*avodas habirurim*)

The achievement of the goal of creation, a "dwelling place" for G-dliness in this lowly world, as this emerges from the writings of Rabbi Schneur Zalman, comes also as the result of a *process*. The every deed of a Jew has a goal - the means of which, the crafting of the deed, is set forth in the *halachos* of Torah - to achieve a specific refinement or sanctification of the creation. In so doing it draws transcendent G-dliness into this world; but this achievement is not yet a "visible" or manifest one. The notion of redemption, as noted above, which comes with the advent of the Messiah and beyond that, with Resurrection of the dead, relates to the completion of the transformation of all the limitations of - each particular *tzimtzum* of - infinite G-dliness within this world. The world must constitute a complete dwelling for transcendent G-dliness, before *Atzmus*, expressed as the transcendent housed within the immanent, is *revealed*.[22]

The Hebrew term for the process of transformation of the world, achieved through conduct guided by mitzvos, is called *avodas habirurim* (the service of refinement or transformation). There are moreover two essential terms, stated in the *Tanya* of Rabbi Schneur Zalman, and elaborated in later chassidic writings, which suggest a "dialectic" in the process of refinement analogous to the notions of externalization and the returning of externalization in Hegel. These are called, in the language of Kabalah, *iscafia* and *is'hapcha*. A Jew, guided by Torah, is led to make an actual imprint of mitzvos on his own material situation, at any given

---

[22] Indeed, according to Maimonides, it is the Messiah who, before being confirmed in the status of Messiah, who actually "pushes" the Jewish people to complete the service of refinement of the world as indicated by *Hilchos M'lochim*, ch. 12.

mitzvos, from the external environment, and from his own time. There is a great resistance to receiving the imprint of internal, bodily "animal" nature, both of which are even to a degree naturally antagonistic to holiness. Accordingly he must *struggle* with his own nature, and must *resist* the seductions of an external world, which is opposed, or are at best indifferent, to sanctity. He must *check* or *bind back* the unholy and this is the sense of *iscafia*, literally "forcing". He works, like the Hegelian servant, engaged in work from which he cannot step back and of which he cannot be free. He is not master of nature, "internal" or external, inasmuch as his whole being is locked in struggle with it, holding it in submission. This is why the *beinoni* - the "intermediate" person, whose service consists principally in *iscafia* - is said to be identified with his animal nature, although he prevails over it by virtue of his G-dly soul. His engagement with it dominates his being: it holds and preoccupies him.

At this point a second stage arrives. It becomes the task of a Jew not simply to hold a world, which is intrinsically antagonistic to spirituality, in check, in abeyance, but actually to transform it. This is the phase of *is'hapcha*, transformation. In *is'hapcha*, both his bodily existence and that part of the world in which the Jew is engaged, is no longer an opponent, albeit held in check, but is actually transformed and appropriated by the realm of holiness: it becomes something holy. The inner bodily nature of the tzaddik - the righteous - individual, whose service is typified by *is'hapcha* is thus called the "flesh of man": that is to say "flesh" - nature - is returned and assimilated to the spiritual identity called "man", becoming one with it.[23] And so it is that *birurim*, deeds of transformation and refinement of creation as a whole - which admit and reveal transcendent G-dliness *within* the finite

---

[23] See *Tanya (Likkutei Amarim)*, ch.29.

Creation (so realizing the manifestation of *Atzmus*, quintessential G-dliness) involve *iscafia* and *is'hapcha*.

Whilst for Hegel the realization of the Absolute becomes concrete in the modern state where it has captured the world for man, its reflective and sovereign master, the vision of Rabbi Schneur Zalman is precisely the inverse. The service of the Jewish people is the vehicle by which quintessential G-dliness will come to manifest Itself as the sole master-occupant of this world. It is through the deeds of the Jewish is the groundwork of the Divine redemption. that redemption is *prepared*, and the renewal of the creation is possible. The "dialectic" of their service of *iscafia* and *is'hapcha* is the groundwork of the *Divine* redemption.

CHAPTER 5

THE INDIVIDUAL AND THE ABSOLUTE
MODERN JEWISH PHILOSOPHY AND THE
PHILOSOPHY OF THE INDIVIDUAL

The trend of the modern, individualist thought of Adorno is not to dissolve the concept of Praxis, the notion that subject and object interact producing a social, economic and cultural complex of relationships. Rather, it rejects the idea that Praxis is logically and intrinsically a "Whole" prior to, and subsuming, the individual within itself. To the contrary, it is individuals who constitute the totality of Praxis, society. The counterpart of this in the Jewish thought of Rabbi Menachem Mendel Schneerson or Rabbi Joseph Ber Soloveitchik is the sense in which the individual through prayer "prompts" Atzmus. The quintessential essence vested in the individual elicits the quintessential Essence above.

If, for Hegel, the manifestation of the Absolute was the fully articulated identity of subject and object, for Adorno this is an impossibility. The infinite "life" of the object, is not amenable to the categories of the subject's "identifying" reason. The subject can apprise the object only through construction, individual and socially uncoerceded, which resists "reification" and permits to exist that which is truly "other" in the object. That alone is the redeemed "identity" of subject and object. In contemporary Jewish thought, Torah is the "expression" of the Absolute, Atzmus. The "giving" of the Torah, the investiture of Atzmus in the individual means that Torah can be "taken" and communicated through the mouthpiece of the individual prophet, sage and even the capable student.

Because, according to Adorno, the truly autonomous individual is not encased within the factual, false totality of social Praxis, he can be a lever of its transformation. For modern Jewish thought, it is because the individual Jew participates in quintessential G-dliness, that he or she is an actual partner in transforming creation: "Israel and the Torah and the Holy One, blessed be He, are all one".

1. The individual as author of reality

The philosophy of the individual

The legacy of the philosophy Hegel, which is fundamental for modern thought, is the notion of the *interaction* or mutual interaction of subject and object. For Hegel reality is the process, the working out of stages and phases, of the subject-object in the context of an "idealist" philosophy. In the writings of the mature Marx, the process of reality became *concrete:* history is the sequence of *material* forms of man's productive relationship with nature.

All this represents the consummation of the Enlightenment's "colonization" of objective reality by the subject "man". Where Adorno and much modern thought takes issue with Hegel, and with previous thought, is in relation to the concept of the "subject" as an *abstract collectivity*. In Hegel, we have seen that subject and object have become two aspects or sides of the one total process. The concept of the *identity* of subject and object, which is associated with the notion of a general subject, similarly becomes problematic in the school of "Young Hegelians" which emerges after the death of Hegel in 1831. There comes to the fore the figure of the *individual* subject. It is the individual who is the real source of social reality. The social whole - subject-object, man-nature as social economy - derives from real, individual human beings. Young Hegelianism, the proto-existentialism of the Danish philosopher Soren Kierkegaard, the liberal individualism which in England led to the Reform Act of 1832 are all species of a new philosophy of the individual as the originator, and not simply the differentiated - individuated - result, of history and society.

Although in his later or "mature" writings, Marx would return to the concept of a collective subject - *class* - reminiscent of the Hegelian total subject-object, in his early work he participates in a typically Young-Hegelian critique of Hegel, which seeks to reverse the relationship of the social or political whole and the individual. In his "Critique of Hegel's Philosophy of the State", Marx notes that for Hegel, the Whole is the subject and the individual a *predicate* or moment of the Whole. The reverse, he states, is true: it is the individual, the supposed predicate who is the real constitutive subject of the State. He writes in his *Economical-philosophical Manuscripts*:

> Above all one must avoid fixing the "society" as an abstraction over against the individual. The individual *is* the *essential social being [das gesellschaftliche Wesen]*. His life expression is . . . an expression and confirmation of the *life of society*.[1]

The foundation and criterion of society is the individual. It is for, and because of, the individual that society exists. He is its *raison d'etre*, its "confirmation", rather than an exemplar, an outcome and representative *of* the social whole.

The philosophy of Theodor Wiesengrund Adorno (1903-1969), the contemporary philosopher, whose work we have here taken to exemplify the modern philosophy of the individual descends in certain ways from Kierkegaard, the Danish philosopher whose work participates in this early generation of individualist thought. Adorno's second academic dissertation *(Habilitationsschrift)*, on Kierkegaard, is devoted to a substantial critique of Kierkegaard's philosophy. Nevertheless the sense of the individual as subject found in Kierkegaard, is fundamental to Adorno's thought. Adorno would state it this way in one of his major works, *Negative Dialektik*:

---

[1] Karl Marx, *Oekonomische-philosophische Manuskripte* (ed. J. Hoeppner), Leipzig: Verlag Philipp Reclam, 1974, p. 187 (present writer's translation).

History has to this day no general subject, however that may be construed. Its substratum is the functional interrelationship of the real individual subjects.[2]

That is to say, although historically individuals have been bound together in various functional - collective, social - relationships, yet the individual is their subject and author. If he has been pressed into a social whole, which appears to negate his historical subjectivity and autonomy, this is because he has *submitted* to it, not because the whole is something *truer* than, or prior to, the individual. Indeed, the perception of this is itself a precondition for the creation of a social order which would express human autonomy:

Only . . . if the totality is recognized as a socially necessary illusion, as the hypostasis of the universal pressed out of individual human beings; if its claim to be absolute is broken - only then will a critical social consciousness retain its freedom to think that things might be different some day.[3]

There is a generality, an organization of individual existences, for human existence is necessarily a *social* one, requiring, as we shall see relationships of exchange, "functional interrelationships". But the generality is the result of the individual subjectivity, and not vice-versa.

The objective side of the whole - that which mediates and interacts with subjectivity - in Hegel was the "metaphysical" notion of substance. In Marx it is nature. This objective side to history - substance or nature - in late Enlightenment thought allows itself, however, to be construed by the subject only in terms of the object's own possibilities, which the subject discovers and establishes. Objectivity - the objectivity of substance or of nature - stands over against, and circumscribes,

---

[2] *Ibid*, p. 279 (present writer's translation).
[3] *Ibid*., p. 297.

the subject. Objectivity - through the organon or instrumentarium of the subject - is determined as, or becomes, what *it* can be. In Adorno's writing, on the other hand, this concept of objectivity is replaced by a notion of *objectification*. It is not substance or nature which, through the activity of the subject, *objectively* discloses itself in a specific sequence of phases or forms, leading for example in Hegel to the present form of political economy and civil society. Rather, it is man, or to use Adorno's phrase, *subjective* (human) *reason* itself which has objectified man's existence in the form it possesses. This notion of objectification is formulated in the writings of Georg Lukacs[4], a thinker whose work bridges the epoch of the late Marx with, and forms an immediate background and source to, Adorno. Here is the concept, that it is not so much nature, but that which man has done with, and made out of nature, which confronts man as an "other". That is to say, through the organon of the scientific, mathematical mind, and its practical extensions, technology and organization and administration, man has *modelled* and *created* an abstract, objective environment. Thus, he fashions a factory work-world, which contains abstract and regimented processes. This is not the objectively necessary way to the things, it is not the sole objective possibility dictated, at any historical juncture, by nature. Rather, it is nature fashioned and reconstituted by man as *second* nature. Lukacs called this *Verdinglichung*, which is translated in English as "reification": making a human relationship, or a relationship with a particular object, *into a thing*, an abstraction, which acquires a reality of its own. Conceptually, in terms of the history of philosophy, *object has become objectification.*

---

[4] *History and Class Consciousness* (transl. R. Livingstone), London: Merlin Press, 2nd ed. 1971. See particularly the Preface to the "New Edition" of 1967.

So it is for Adorno that the individual is both the *subject* of history and society, as well as the author of the *objective* conditions mediating his subjective (choosing, free) existence, namely the reified structures of society. It is not a "contradiction" that the individual creates an objective abstraction - "functional relationships" - over against himself. It is objectification - reification - which makes society possible. The relationship of the individual subject and society as a reified whole, form which the individual receives his identity, has been put by Adorno also in terms of the interrelationship of the particular and the general.

> The aspect of individuality *[Einzelmenschlichkeit]*, called by Schelling "*Egoitaet*", cannot be discounted from any concept of the subject . . . Conversely, as soon as there is reflection in a general conceptual form upon the individual, not only the "this here" of some particular person is involved, [but also] the individual is made into a generality similar to that which was explicit in the idealist concept of the subject; even the expression "particular person" requires the species-concept *[Gattungsbegriff]*; otherwise, it would be devoid of meaning. The proper name has implicit in it the relationship to the general. [5]

Objectifying or "identifying" reason, which tends to subsume the radically particular, the individual, within general concepts, translates in *social* terms into a concept of "exchange". The phenomenon of "exchange" in Adorno stands over and regulates the individual, contrary to his living particularity. The market society establishes a systematic means for "the abstract comparability of [human beings']

---

[5] "*Zu Subjekt und Objekt*" in Stichworte (Frankfurt am Main: Suhrkamp, 1969), p. 151

social labour"[6]. It classes people into categories and strata of activity. In its "exchange" the market establishes the relations of equivalence and commensurability - price - between distinct species of labour or commodity production; between these categories people are sortable, within them, interchangeable. This sense of exchange, as "fungibility" or interchangeability is explored and criticized by Adorno in its extreme forms in a variety of spheres of society. As the form of objective social mediation, it is, however, an unavoidable mechanism:

> So little as the social mediation [cf. reification] could exist without the mediated, without the elements - individual human beings, individual institutions, individual situations - so little do these exist without mediation.[7]

The "whole" of society, defined by Hegel as subject-object, is for Adorno in both its subjective and objective sides, the work of individual human authorship - of subjective human autonomy and human objectifying reason.

Prayer - the invocation of *Atzmus*

In the previous chapter we sought to show the Jewish parallel to the secular notion of historical *process* - the dialectic of subjectivity and objectivity in the *one* subject-object - in the concept of the Divine act of creation. It is *Atzmus*, quintessential G-dliness, which "comprises" and coordinates both infinite, engendering ("objective") and delimiting ("subjective") powers in order to create. This, however, is quintessential G-dliness reflected in the creation, or more

---

[6] *Gesellschaft", Gesammelte Schriften, Bd.* 8 (Frankfurt am Main: Suhrkamp, 1972), p.13.

[7] *Ibid,,* p. 11

[8] Though it must be reiterated: not that these "inhere" in - in the sense of defining - *Atzmus*, but rather that they are originated by *Atzmus*.

specifically in the continuous act of creation. It does not yet explicitly direct us to *Atzmus* as *Creator*. Why does G-d, comprehended as Creator, decide to create this and not something else? Why now and not later? We speak here of the *will* - the *decision*, so to speak - to create. Or, if these questions cannot be answered about quintessential G-dliness *Itself*, can then man relate to this level of Divine will in the sense of being able to invoke or *prompt* the act of creation, which is G-d's choice and decision? For if man can, within the boundaries and the goals which G-d has determined for the creation, "prompt" G-d to create - to decide to create in this way and not in another - it would tell us something also about man: that he is, in some sense, a partner in creation, a "creator".

In the writings of two major modern Jewish thinkers, Rabbi Menachem Mendel Schneerson (1902-1994) - known simply as the Lubavitcher Rebbe - and Rabbi Joseph B. Soloveitchik (1903-1993), we find analysis of a "covenantal" relationship between the Jewish people and G-d, and its association with the particular efficacy of *prayer*. The essential characteristic of prayer, as explained by the Lubavitcher Rebbe, is found in the formula *(nusach)* frequently found in prayer, "May it be Your will . . ."[9]. It is explained that the sense of this is that, even if the Creator has already ordained things to be in such and such way, the supplicant in prayer asks that G-d *will it to be differently*. The notion is illustrated by the story of a particular Sage who was so poor that he was informed by his wife one Sabbath eve that there was no oil for the Sabbath lights. Observing that there was vinegar in the house, he said, "May the One who commanded oil to burn, command the vinegar to burn". And so it was[10]. The sage wanted to fulfill the *Divine* commandment of kindling the Sabbath lights. What he prayed

---

[9] See *Likkutei Sichos*, Vol. 10, p.38.
[10] Talmud Tractate *Ta'anis* 25a.

for was that the impediment in the order of creation to fulfillment of this Divine purpose, be *removed*.

That which enables a Jew to elicit, so to speak, a "change" in the ordering of creation for the ultimate fulfillment of the Divine purpose is the special nature of the bond between the Jewish people and G-d, established by the "choice" of G-d of the Jewish people at Sinai. One of the themes most strongly elaborated in the writings of the Lubavitcher Rebbe is the nature of this Divine choice with all its ramifications. Now already Rabbi Schneur Zalman of Liadi had written that the souls of the Jewish people are a "part" of quintessential "G-d is bound utterly to G-d, even though consciously a Jew may not be aware of this. G-d has committed Himself to the ultimate redemption of every Jew, through the ineluctable mechanisms which lead ultimately to the highest form of redemption, the resurrection of the dead, as the Mishnah states, that "every Jew has a share in the world to come" as consequent upon this commitment, constitutes a "bonding" of quintessential G-dliness which associates the Jewish people in a manner of an indestructible mutual commitment: the essence of a Jew is bound utterly to G-d, even though consciously a Jew may not be aware of this. G-d has committed Himself to the ultimate redemption of every Jew, through the ineluctable mechanisms which lead ultimately to the highest form of redemption, the resurrection of the dead, as the *Mishnah* states, that "*every* Jew has a share in the world to come"[13]. G-d has chosen, "invested Himself", so to speak, in, the Jewish people - not just in their souls, but also in their *persons*.[14]

---

[11] *Tanya (Likkutei Amarim)*, ch. 2.

[12] *Likkutei Sichos*, Vol. 4, p. 1309 fn. 1.

[13] Talmud Tractate *Sanhedrin* 90a.

[14] *Tanya, Likkutei Amarim*, ch. 49, as elucidated in *Likkutei Sichos*, Vol. 23, p. 219.

It is part of the Divine intention - of *Atzmus* - that the Jewish people should be the agency of the redemptive transformation of the creation. Accordingly, the material needs and situation with which a Jew carries out this agency, are the principal object of prayer[15] and "touch" *Atzmus* Itself. [16] Now, when quintessential G-dliness chose the persons of the Jewish people, that Quintessentiality became so to speak the being of the Jew him or herself, for "where Essence is drawn down it is impossible that there should be a hold for anything else"[17]. This "oneness" - this profound identity and bonding of the Jewish people with Quintessential G-dliness - creates that commonality which makes it possible for essence "below" (the Jew) to arouse Essence "above", and a Jew is able so to speak, to persuade *Atzmus* to create that which was not previously "intended". Just as a child, by virtue of its special privity or intimacy with its father, can arouse in him a decision to alter the means towards bringing the good which the father wants for the child, so too in prayer, one is able to ask G-d that conditions which may have been previously ordained, be *changed*, for the sake of fulfillment of Divine redemptive purpose.

Whilst the Lubavitcher Rebbe comprehends this union of the individual Jew with quintessential G-dliness as the result of the choice of *G-d* in the Jewish people at Sinai, Rabbi Joseph B. Soloveitchik looks at this from the point of view of the *quest of the individual Jew* for this relationship. The idea is common to both: it relates to the bonding of man and G-d, which Rabbi Soloveitchik calls a relationship of "covenant". The initial covenantal relationship between G-d and man, which prepares

---

[15] The *shmoneh esrei*, the centre piece of Jewish prayer, being largely concerned with requesting of practical, material needs.

[16] See *Likkutei Sichos*, Vol. 19, pp. 291-97.

[17] *Likkutei Sichos*, Vol. 23, p. 219.

the Jewish people as a vehicle for the Divine word, prophecy, and its own ethico-moral charge or mission, is prayer. This is set out pre-eminently in the essay *"The Lonely Man of Faith"*. The essay begins by considering the two accounts of the creation of man in *Genesis*. The first account is where we find that he is created together with Eve and the injunction is given to them to subdue the world. In the second account he is alone, and it is further related how he was created from the earth and how G-d breathed into him a living soul[18]. The first is elaborated by Rabbi Soloveitchik as a portrait of a fully socialized "majestic man", poised for technical conquest of the creation. The second portrait is that of man, seeking a spiritual and human community, emerging from an existential "loneliness". These represent two dimensions of human existence. It is the second dimension, from which spirituality springs, that is the topic of *"The Lonely Man of Faith"*.

In this dimension, the absolute particularity of his own existence and of existence in general arouses within man an awe for the *living* like the child who "seeks the unusual and wonderful in every ordinary thing and event"[19]. But it is lonely. This loneliness is not alleviated by his technical conquests and social and cultural achievements. In the midst of the absolute singularity of his existence, he seeks to emerge from loneliness and to embrace the Transcendent, G-d. And this is faith: "the intrusion of the eternal upon the temporal"[20]. There is thus fashioned the covenantal prayer relationship. The essential *foundation* of this relationship is man's *submission* to G-d, to the extent that he is *overpowered* by G-d. The pre-eminent

---

[18] There are further differences. See Rabbi J.B. Soloveitchik, "The Lonely Man of Faith", in L.D. Stitskin (ed.), *Studies in Judaica in Honor of Dr. Samuel Belkin as Scholar and Educator*, N.Y: K'tav and Yeshiva University Press,1974, pp. 74-5.

[19] *Ibid.*, p. 80.

[20] *Ibid.* p. 116

symbol of this, it would seem, according to Rabbi Soloveitchik, similarly to the Lubavitcher Rebbe, the experience of the giving of the Torah at Sinai, concerning which the talmudic agada states, G-d "held the mountain over the heads" of the Jewish people and told them that if they would not accept it, they would be buried there. Faith's "essence is characterized by fixity and enduring identity."[21]

From the singular relationship of man with G-d is thus formed a covenantal faith *community*, a many. It arises from the prayer of the individual inasmuch as the individual experiences sympathy for the travail of others, and offers the "petition" of the many.[22]

Rabbi Soloveitchik speaks of the covenantal relationship as "redemptive"[23]:

> Only when G-d emerged from He-anonymity into the illumined spaces of community-knowability and charged man with an ethico-moral mission, did Adam *absconditus* and Eve *abscondita*, while revealing themselves to G-d in prayer and in unqualified commitment - also reveal themselves to each other in sympathy and love on the one hand and common action on the other. Thus the final objective of the human quest for redemption was attained; the individual felt relieved from loneliness and isolation. The community of the committed became, *ipso facto*, a community of friends - not of neighbors or acquaintances.[24]

In these modern Jewish philosophies, the individual's task is thus to fashion community; and, as explained in Chassidic thought, the community of the Jewish people takes in

---

[21] *Ibid.*, p.116
[22] *Ibid.*, p. 97.
[23] *Ibid.*, p. 118.
[24] *Ibid.*, 101.

ultimately the entire "world" inasmuch as every Jew relates to a part of world and the totality of those parts make up the totality of the world. That is, the individual affects the collectivity of the Jewish people and beyond this the entire creation, as the Lubavticher Rebbe adapts and extends the words of the Medrash:

"Just as the Holy One blessed be he creates worlds, so does Ya'akov create worlds" - to the extent that one may say that the existence of the worlds departs on a [single] Jew through his learning Torah and fulfillment of its mitzvos.[25]

For both the Lubavitcher Rebbe and Rabbi Soloveitchik, the bond or covenant which prayer activates, "brings in" G-d, it elicits specific Divine response. Man is a partner - "has a say" - in the act of creation. Here is the difference with Adorno, for whom the individual is the *engineer* of both subjective and objective dimensions - the whole - of reality, reconstituted as society. For in Adorno man is truly alone, whilst for the Jewish philosophers, G-d creates - directs and redirects the creation towards redemption - in covenant with man.

2. Apprising the Absolute

Non-conceptual construction

In view of Adorno's concept that the "false" totality is achieved through the *activity* of the subject, so it must then also be that the normative, accomplished "identity" of subject and object - the manifestation of the *Absolute* - is also achieved by human constructive reason and activity. This would appear *paradoxical*. For, in contradistinction to Hegel, Adorno starts from the *non-identity* of subject and object. Subject is by definition conceptual; object is the "other", the non-conceptual

---

[25] *Sichos Kodesh, loc. cit.*

realm of being, life itself. The task of the subject is therefore not to impose its own limited reason on object, but to attempt a "reconciliation" of subject and object. This is not the surrender of the subject's conceptual and constructive apparatus and its self-dissolution before the object, the *mimesis* characteristic of animism[26]. The subject must use its reason: it must construct, objectify. And yet *within this construction*, it must seek to overcome its own limitations and attempt mimesis, unqualified exposure of the construct of reason to the object. This is Adorno's ideal of *"ueber den Begriff durch den Begriff hinauszugelangen"* ("by means of the concept to get beyond the concept")[27], whereby the genuinely distinct or different character of each and all things could yet be "conceptualized". The true adequation - identity and reconciliation - of subject and object is thus to be achieved by this paradoxical "construction" which seeks to transcend itself: subject approaches and "adequates" that which is wholly unlike - non-identical to - it.

The model of representation - "identification" - which overcomes itself, achieving *some kind of* mimesis with and through the moment of formal rationality and construction, is to be found for Adorno in the *authentic* art work (and so too in the realm of critical, as distinct from non-critical theory, which is ideology). Art is an enclave which appears to have been protected to a degree from the general, totalizing trend of reification:

> In the general development . . . art has something of the suspicious mortgage of that which has not fully come along . . . In that which is conserved in art and which art unconditionally requires, there is gathered what . . . was violently cut away by civilization. [What was torn away and]

---

[26] See Chapter 1, section 1.
[27] *Negative Dialektik*, p.25

repressed, together with the suffering of human-kind under that which was forced from them, no doubt expresses itself in the primary forms of mimesis.[28]

Adorno writes that "aesthetic conduct is the unenfeebled corrective to the reified consciousness"[29]. Art anticipates a condition in which, to quote Adorno, the object, nature, is engaged technically but through a construction which *assists*, rather than crippling, individual subjectivity.[30]

Analogous to the objectifying structures of thought are those of society, reified in the manner (in Adorno's sense) of "exchange". Here, too, the *ideal* is a society which, within the identities and equivalences furnished by the categories of social labour under the principle of "exchange", yet enables the individual to preserve his difference and particularity. This Adorno calls in one place "the ideal of free and just exchange":

Critique of the exchange principle as the identifying [principle] of thought wants the ideal of free and just exchange, until today merely a pretext, to be realized. That alone would transcend exchange. If the Critical Theory had

---

[28] *Aesthetische Theorie*, Frankfurt am Main: Suhrkamp, 1970, p. 487.

[29] *Ibid.*, p. 488

[30] "Utility *[das Nuetzliche]* would be a highest ideal, the thing become human, the reconciliation with the objects which no longer create a wall against human beings and bring ignominy upon them. The perception of technical things in childhood, in relation to which they stand as something close and helping, clean of the profit interest, promises such a condition. The conception was not strange to the social utopias. The vanishing point of the development could be thought of in terms that the completely utilitarian things lost their coldness. Not only would human beings no longer have to suffer under the thing-like character of the world: similarly the things would experience their own [essential realization] as soon as they completely found their purpose, redeemed from their own thing-likeness [reified objectivity]". *'Funktionalismus heute'*, *Ohne Leitbild. Parva aesthetica.* Frankfurt am Main: Suhrkamp, 1967, p.123

revealed it as the [exchange] of equal things [which are] in fact unequal, so too, the critique of the unequal in the equal aims also at equality, remaining fully sceptical of the rancour in the bourgeois ideal of equality which tolerates nothing qualitatively different. If no part of the [individuality of the] living labour of any person were kept from him, then rational Identity would be reached and society would have passed beyond identifying thought.[31]

Thus, although reification necessarily mediates the life of the individual, there is envisaged the construction of a form of free social exchange, the true or rational identity of subject and object (or, for Adorno, of instrumental reason and the *life* of man and nature) - the traditional goal of philosophy. This "Absolute" Adorno calls a "*Miteinander des Verschiedenen*" ("togetherness of the different").[32]

In short, reality – the mesh of subject and object - awaits emancipation through the work of man. Utopia is to be constructed. But that the *task* of "reconciling" subject with object, "identifying reason" with the "non-identical", should be left to the subject *itself* is a contradiction which ultimately vitiates Adorno's "critical theory" on its own terms.

The mouthpiece of Divine speech

Both the Lubavitcher Rebbe and Rabbi Soloveitchik portray the world of Torah, as something which essentially belongs, perfect in itself, in a realm wholly removed from creation. In this sense the Sages spoke metaphorically of the Torah "preceding the world by two thousand years"[33]: not a precedence in time, for time does not exist before creation, but

---

[31] *Negative Dialektik*, p. 148.
[32] *Ibid.*, p.151.
[33] *B'reishis Rabba* 8:2.

a precedence in spiritual level. It is rather an *olam m'vurar*, a refined and perfected world, to use the words of the Lubavitcher Rebbe, or in the terms of Rabbi Soloveitchik, an "ideal world", the ideal world of *halachah*.

The distinctness of the Torah consists in the sense that the Torah is G-d's, it is not the work of man. The first word of the Ten Commandments - I (am the L-rd your G-d) - in Hebrew is *A-No-CHi*. This is interpreted homiletically as an acrostic of the words *Ana c'sovis yehavis*: "[My] "I" - I wrote, I gave'[34]. G-d has "given" - inscribed - Himself in Torah so to speak. Not that G-d was compelled to give this Torah rather than another, but just as, on a worldly and profane plane, an artist could be said (not to have *defined*, but) to have *expressed* his essence in an artwork, or in a writing, so it is that G-dliness is reflected and expressed in Torah. It is G-d's expression, communication to the creation, such that the grasping of Torah by a human intellect affords a union with the Divine. The precepts of the Torah, with their halachos, are the forms through which the creation is *made* into a vehicle for G-dliness. The *study* of the precepts enables in the faculties of the mind the *experience* of, or *attachment* to, G-dliness[35]. The *Author*, the *Speaker* of the Torah is the Jewish concept of the Absolute: *Atzmus*, quintessential G-dliness.

Inasmuch as the Torah is an expression of *Atzmus*, it follows that it cannot be apprehended by an ordinary act of human understanding. A Jew has the ability to become the recipient, the *mouthpiece* of Torah, whether in prophecy or, at another level, in halachah. This ability follows, for the Lubavitcher Rebbe, from the investiture of *Atzmus* in the Jewish people at

---

[34] Talmud Tractate *Shabbos* 105a.
[35] This point was made to me by Rabbi Y. Winner. The significance of the giving of the Torah is not (only, or so much) *what* was said, but *Who* said it.

the giving of the Torah at Sinai. The quintessential attachment and spiritual commonality between G-d and the Jewish people, achieved then, makes it possible for a Jew to access and express the quintessential wisdom or "expression" of G-dliness. In the words of the Lubavitcher Rebbe, the effect of the *giving* of the Torah is that when Jews learn and enunciate new insights in Torah, their words are the *words of G-d*. The Jew, whether in earlier generations of prophetic greatness or in recent, lowly epochsd the Jewish people. Prayer and prophecy are alternate relationships between man and G-d:icle for Divine wisdom. That is to say, he is actually *uttering* Divine speech.[36]

For Rabbi Soloveitchik prophecy, or alternatively the ability of the Jew to reveal halachah, is the other side of the covenantal relationship between G-d and the Jewish people. Prayer and prophecy are alternate relationships between man and G-d:

> In short, prayer and prophecy are two synonymous designations of the covenantal G-d-man colloquy . . . The difference between prayer and prophecy is . . . related not to the substance of the dialogue but rather to the order in which it is conducted. While within the prophetic community G-d takes the initiative - He speaks and man listens - in the prayer community the initiative belongs to man: he does the speaking and G-d, the listening. The word of prophecy is G-d's and is accepted by man.[37]

Prayer "ascends"; Divine revelation - which comes through man - "descends" in response to it: it comes as a manifestation of Divine will, "*ipso facto* G-d's law and norm"[38]:

---

[36] "*U's'fartem lochem*", *Sefer HaMa'amarim 5744*, Brooklyn, N.Y., 5740 p.159.
[37] "*The Lonely Man of Faith*", p.95.
[38] *Ibid.*, p. 98.

Prayer must always be related to a prayerful life which is consecrated to the realization of the Divine imperative and, as such it is not a separate entity, but the sublime prologue to Halachic action.[39]

In Adorno the project of apprehending the "Absolute" constructing the reconciliation, or the paradoxical "identity", of subject and object, founders on the impossible desideratum that the *subject* with its own limited, immanent categories, should in some way be able to bring into equation subjectivity and objectivity, immanence and transcendence. In the Jewish thought of the Lubavitcher Rebbe and Rabbi Soloveitchik, *Atzmus* - the Orchestrator and Reconciler of transcendence and immanence - the Absolute speaks and expresses *Itself* through the human mouthpieces of prophecy and halachah. Through Torah *Atzmus*, the "Absolute" is *received*: in the words of the Midrash[40], with Torah, it is "Me [Whom] you are taking".

3. The individual and redemption

Praxis

The sense of the individual is brought out most generally in Adorno's thought in a theory of social action or *praxis*, which is far more radical than that of Marx and, needless to say, of Hegel. The sense of human action in the philosophies of Hegel and Marx is to be found in the notion of the interaction of subject and object. Subject construes, works upon object. But what is subject? It is man or mind, but it is an aggregate concept of man or mind. Because subject is a whole, and is moreover part of a larger whole, the whole of subject-object, it bears the anonymity of process. Thus for Hegel, the subject is

---

[39] *Ibid.*, p. 100.
[40] *Vayikra Rabba* 30:13. Quoted in *Likkutei Sichos*, Vol. 33, p. 33.

an abstraction, *Weltgeist*, of which the individual is simply an exemplar, a bearer. And so too, in Marx, who spoke so much of "audacious human will": the subject is really *history* and social-historical process. In Adorno's work, on the other hand, one has the concept of the social whole, in which reality is the construction of *individuals*. The individual is not a representative of an historical or world-intellectual process; he or she is the concrete *maker* - or one of the many individual makers - of that whole. This is the deepest sense of *making* or *doing*: that there is an identifiable doer, rather than one, whose doing is ascribed to, and is bound up with (or is simply the individuated result of) a higher historical process. And if a whole has arisen which shows a complete regimentation of human individualities into a total system, which contradicts individual autonomy, that itself is only proof of the "falsity" and "ideological" character of a society, to which individuals have *submitted* and repressed their individualities.

It is, moreover, the *individual's* activity which can adapt practice to theory: which is able to break through the false totality and to create the emancipated order, responsive to, and permeated, by "individualities". If, for Hegel and Marx, material and intellectual realities simply mirror one another, in Adorno a certain primacy, in an emancipative sense, is given to the intellectual realm, thought and art. Here individualism and individual interventions are more readily registered. In thought or art, there begins the critique which can change society. For whilst social and intellectual forms unavoidably mediate the artwork, and so too critical thinking, their conscious goal is also to remember the idea of mimesis: of receiving the objective as it is, beyond the subject. They intimate the reconciliation of subject and object, but do so negatively: in the reified and formal-rational elements which they necessarily absorb from the subject's reason, they seek to reveal the "other", the dissonances or breaks between reality and concept. Their task is, using concept, to perceive the *resistance* of reality to the concept employed by the subject, and in these resistances to relate to the object.

Only because no artwork can emphatically succeed do its forces become released; only through this does it glimpse the reconciliation. Art is rationality, which criticizes this [rationality] without leaving it"[41].

The artwork and so too critical thought thus shows how the subject's relationship to the things might be. In social terms, it envisages and points to "just exchange". In its critical role, art actually redeems reality. The artwork *places* - reconstructs - socialized, objectified reality *now* in the light of its redemption.[42] This follows from the rigorous concept of praxis, individual formative activity, in Adorno's philosophy. Thought is not a reflection of reality, one side of a total historical process, of subject-object. Thought itself is an *act*. It seizes the world, deals with the world *practically*. Adorno wrote in the essay, *"Marginalien zu Theorie und Praxis"*: "Thought is a doing, theory is a form of praxis . . ."[43] True critical thinking is least of all a reflex of society. The praxis *of* theory is one of the freest realms of praxis and for this reason it is also the most efficacious.

The practice of critical theory and art, which actually transforms society - socialized nature - and makes it come to its emancipatory potential, is essentially the work of individuals. For since art and critical theory occupy enclaves which have resisted total reification, they possess the reserve or creative space, from which the individual is able to work to transform society. This seizes the truth that the social whole

---

[41] *Aesthetische Theorie*, p. 87.
[42] See T.W. Adorno, *"Zum Ende"* in *Minima Moralia*, Frankfurt am Main: Suhrkamp, 1971.
[43] *Stichworte*, Frankfurt am Main: Suhrkamp, 1969, p.163.

exists only for the sake of the individual, who must be free within it, to penetrate, permeate and shape it.[44]

Man as creator

The picture of the individual in the writings of the Lubavticher Rebbe and Rabbi Soloveitchik in certain ways resembles that of Adorno. In a talk given in 1981[45], which was actually attended by Rabbi Soloveitchik, and which strongly demonstrates points of convergence between both thinkers' work, the Lubavitcher Rebbe stated that the individual Jew is able to transform the creation in its entirety. This is achieved in that he or she employs the power of the mitzvos of the Torah, which is "master over the world", in addressing and dealing with the world, so that every Jew is a "master" over creation. Here the Lubavitcher Rebbe illustrates a notion developed elsewhere[47] that man is a "partner in the work of creation". This indeed is why man was originally created alone: to demonstrate to him that he is balanced against the creation in its entirety, and that it "belongs" to him as an individual. It is true that subsequently the Jewish people emerges as a multiciplicty of individuals, each with his or her own "portion", or sphere of activity and influence, in the world. Yet the lesson from the solitary creation of man is that it is placed in the hands of the individual, via his service in his own portion, to bring the creation into its redeemed unity with G-d.

The transformative work of the individual Jew takes place through a process of *his'chadshus*, renewal. The meaning of

---

[44] See *Aesthetische Theorie*, pp. 452-453.
[45] Rabbi Menachem Mendel Schneerson, *Sichos Kodesh* (unedited transcripts of talks), Talk of 10 Sh'vat, 5740.
[46] According to reports of those present.
[47] *Likkutei Sichos*, Vol. 6, pp. 22-23, fn. 73.

this is that, in the words of the Lubavitcher Rebbe, it is within the ability of Jews to take the material and cultural phenomena of their environment, and even though it represent something indifferent or even antagonistic to G-dliness, yet *reconstitute* it as a fitting *vehicle* for G-dliness. The object, world, becomes or is made into the *object of mitzvos*[48]. This is compared to the process of creation *ex nihilo*, in that it takes something which represents a "negative existence", or an "existence of absence," as impurity or non-sanctity is termed, in that it has no enduring power, and converts it into an object of sanctity. Impurity has no power of endurance; sanctity is a true, viable existence: it is cumulative and enduring by definition. Consequently the act of reconstitution and renewal through Torah and mitzvos, makes something which is "not" into something which "is", and this is like Divine creation of "something" from "nothing".[49]

The archetypal Jew, with whom Rabbi Soloveitchik deals in one of his few published works is "halachic man". Whilst this refers to a scholarly Jew, it is in greater or lesser measure the significance of every Jew. This task of halachic man is "the redemption of the world . . . via the adaptation of empirical

---

[48] "Some objects themselves become holiness or the objects of mitzvos, or appurtenances of holiness and appurtenances of mitzvos. Below this, however, when a Jew acts simply "for the sake of Heaven", or in a manner of " knowing Him in all your paths" [a Jew similarly affects the Creation]. There are aspects of the Creation which are simply preconditional, or pre-preconditional [to holiness and mitzvos]. This goes even further, to the point where there is no direct or manifest link between them and Jews and Torah: it is simply that through an action with an individual of a species, there is brought about an elevation in the entire species . . ." *Likkutei Sichos*, Vol. 26, p.65.

[49] *Likkutei Sichos*, Vol. 6, pp. 22-23, fn. 73.

reality to the ideal patterns of Halakhah"[50]. This is achieved by man through the virtually G-dly powers to which he can come. Lawrence Kaplan notes, in this regard, "the adjectives that Rabbi Soloveitchik uses to describe the personality of the halakhic scholar are very revealing: master, powerful, creator, autonomous, independent, etc."[51] In short, some sense of *Atzmus*, as Chassidus speaks of this, the quintessential creative power and role of the Creator, has been installed in the Jew.

The Lubavitcher Rebbe dwells greatly on points elaborated by Rabbi Schneur Zalman in his *Tanya*: upon the level and nature of the Jewish soul, which derives from *Atzmus*[52]; upon how at this level, all the Jewish people are *one* essence rooted in absolute and quintessential G-dliness, it being simply that parts of this essence have descended into different bodies[53], and have so been allocated to influence different portions of creation. In the words of the Ba'al Shem Tov, moreover, "The [nature of an] essence [is that] when you take hold of part of it, you take hold of all of it.[54]" This means that the spiritual being - quintessential G-dliness - of the Jewish people, is vested in the *individual* Jew, and gives him or her, his or her extraordinary creative and transformative power. At the level of essence, the part is *proof* of the Whole. Each Jew, as a part of the one essential spiritual entity of the Jewish people - bonded with *Atzmus* and with Torah - has it within his or her

---

[50] Rabbi J.B. Soloveitchik, *Halakhic Man* (transl. Lawrence Kaplan), Philadeplphia: Jewish Publication Society of America, 1983, p.37.

[51] *"The Religious Philosophy of Rabbi Joseph Soloveitchik"*, *Tradition*, Vol. 12, No. 2, p.52.

[52] *Likkutei Amarim*, ch. 2.

[53] *Ibid.*, ch. 32.

[54] Quoted in *Likkutei Sichos*, Vol. 3, p. 825. To employ a possible analogy, we cannot necessarily detain a person by seizing his jacket, but we can by holding on to his little finger, which is *part* of him.

power to redeem the entire world. Maimonides stated this when he ruled that each Jew should view the world as a scales balanced between exile and redemption, which with one good deed (or word or thought) he could tip towards redemption.[55] The metaphor is stated not simply to *motivate* a Jew in his or her service. This one individual - with his one deed - *can* tip the scales. The "individual is the many".[56]

[55] *Hilchos T'shuvah* 3:4.
[56] *Sichos Kodesh, loc. cit.*